J. R. Trotter

The School Law of West Virginia and Opinions of the Attorney-General and Decisions of the State Superintendent of Free Schools

J. R. Trotter

The School Law of West Virginia and Opinions of the Attorney-General and Decisions of the State Superintendent of Free Schools

ISBN/EAN: 9783337865146

Printed in Europe, USA, Canada, Australia, Japan

Cover: Foto ©Suzi / pixelio.de

More available books at **www.hansebooks.com**

THE
SCHOOL LAW

OF

WEST VIRGINIA

AND

OPINIONS OF THE ATTORNEY-GENERAL AND DECISIONS OF THE STATE SUPERINTENDENT OF FREE SCHOOLS

With Explanations and Forms.

REVISED AND ARRANGED BY
J. R. TROTTER,
STATE SUPERINTENDENT OF FREE SCHOOLS.

CHARLESTON :
WILL E. FORSYTH, PUBLIC PRINTER,
1897.

CONSTITUTIONAL PROVISIONS

RELATING TO THE

School System of West Virginia.

ARTICLE IV.

*　　*　　*　　*　　*　　*

5. Every person elected or appointed to any office, Oath of office. before proceeding to exercise the authority, or discharge the duties thereof, shall make oath or affirmation that he will support the Constitution of the United States and the Constiution of this State, and that he will faithfully discharge the duties of his said office to the best of his skill and judgment; and no other oath, declaration, or test shall be required as a qualification, unless herein otherwise provided.

6. All officers elected or appointed under this Consti- Removal from tution, may, unless in cases herein otherwise provided office. for, be removed from office for official misconduct, incompetence, neglect of duty, or gross immorality, in such manner as may be prescribed by general laws, and unless so removed, they shall continue to discharge the duties of their respective offices, until their successors are elected, or appointed and qualified.

*　　*　　*　　*　　*　　*

8. The Legislature, in cases not provided for in this Legislature to Constitution, shall prescribe by general laws, the terms prescribe of office, powers, duties and compensation of all public terms of office officers and agents, and the manner in which they shall be elected, appointed and removed.

ARTICLE VIII.

27. Each county shall be laid off into districts, not Districts. less than three nor more than ten in number, and as nearly equal as may be in territory and population. *　　*　　*

ARTICLE IX.

*   *   *   *   *

County officers subject to indictment.

4. The Presidents of the County Courts, the Justices of the Peace, Sheriffs, Prosecuting Attorneys, Clerks of the Circuit and of the County Courts, and all other county officers, shall be subject to indictment for malfeasance, misfeasance, or neglect of official duty, and on conviction thereof, their offices shall become vacant.

I. I am inclined to the opinion that the words "all other county officers." as used in this section, include members of boards of education, although they are elected in districts. This is by no means clear, however. This section is in force *ex proprio vigore* and needs no additional legislation.— *Alfred Caldwell, Attorney-General.*

ARTICLE X.

*   *   *   *   *

Capitation tax.

2. The Legislature shall levy an annual capitation tax of one dollar upon each male inhabitant of the State who has attained the age of twenty-one years, which shall be annually appropriated to the support of Free Schools. Persons afflicted with bodily infirmity may be exempted from this tax.

*   *   *   *   *

Power of Legislature to levy.

5. The power of taxation of the Legislature shall extend to provisions for the payment of the State debt, and interest thereon, the support of free schools, and the payment of the annual estimated expenses of the State; but whenever any deficiency in the revenue shall exist in any year, it shall, at the regular session thereof held next after the deficiency occurs, levy a tax for the ensuing year, sufficient with the other sources of income, to meet such deficiency, as well as the estimated expenses of such year.

*   *   *   *   *   *

County taxes not to exceed etc.

7. County authorities shall never assess taxes, in any one year, the aggregate of which shall exceed ninety-five cents per hundred dollars valuation, except for the support of free schools; payment of indebtedness existing at the time of the adoption of this Constitution; and for the payment of any indebtedness with the interest thereon, created under the succeeding section, unless such assessment, with all questions involving the increase of such aggregate, shall have been submitted to the vote of the people of the county, and have received three-fifths of all the votes cast for and against it.

See Brannon vs. County Court, 33 W. Va., p. 789, construing this section.

8. No county, city, school district, or municipal corporation, except in cases where such corporations have already authorized their bonds to be issued, shall hereafter be allowed to become indebted, in any manner, or for any purpose, to an amount, including existing indebtedness in the aggregate, exceeding five per centum on the value of the taxable property therein to be ascertained by the last assessment for State and county taxes, previous to the incurring of such indebtedness; nor without, at the same time providing for the collection of a direct annual tax, sufficient to pay, annually, the interest on such debt, and the principal thereof, within, and not exceeding thirty-four years; *Provided,* That no debt shall be contracted under this section, unless all questions connected with the same, shall have been first submitted to a vote of the people, and received three-fifths of all the votes cast for and against the same.

[margin: Bonded indebtedness.]
[margin: No debt except by vote of people.]

ARTICLE XII.

1. The Legislature shall provide by general law, for a thorough and efficient system of Free Schools.

See 4 W. Va., p. 499.

2. The State Superintendent of Free Schools shall have a general supervision of free schools, and perform such other duties in relation thereto as may be prescribed by law. If in the performance of any such duty imposed upon him by the Legislature, he shall incur any expenses, he shall be reimbursed therefor; *Provided,* The amount does not exceed five hundred dollars in any one year.

[margin: General supervision.]

3. The Legislature may provide for county superintendents, and such other officers as may be necessary to carry out the objects of this Article, and define their duties, powers and compensation.

[margin: County superintendents.]

4. The existing permanent and invested school fund, and all money accruing to this State from forfeited, delinquent, waste and unappropriated lands; and from lands heretofore sold for taxes and purchased by the State of Virginia, if hereafter redeemed or sold to others than this State; all grants, devises or bequests that may be made to this State for the purposes of education or where the purposes of such grants, devises or bequests are not specified; this State's just share of the literary fund of Virginia, whether paid over or otherwise liquidated; and any sums of money, stocks, or property, which this State shall have the right to claim from the

[margin: School Fund.]

State of Virginia for educational purposes; the proceeds of the estates of persons who may die without leaving a will or heir, and of all escheated lands; the proceeds of any taxes that may be levied on the revenues of any corporation; all moneys that may be paid as an equivalent for exemption from military duty; and such sums as may, from time to time, be appropriated by the Legislature for the purpose, shall be set apart as a separate fund to be called the "School Fund," and invested under such regulation as may be prescribed by law, in the interest bearing securities of the United States, or of this State, or if such interest bearing securities cannot be obtained, then said "School Fund" shall be invested in such other solvent interest bearing securities as shall be approved by the Governor, Superintendent of Free Schools, Auditor and Treasurer, who are hereby constituted the "Board of the School Fund," to manage the same under such regulations as may be prescribed by law; and the interest thereof shall be annually applied to the support of Free Schools throughout the State, and to no other purpose whatever. But any portion of said interest remaining unexpended at the close of the fiscal year shall be added to, and remain a part of, the capital of the "School Fund"; *Provided*, That all taxes which shall be received by the State upon delinquent lands, except the taxes due to the State thereon, shall be refunded to the county, or district by or for which the same were levied.

Board of the School Fund. *(margin note)*

Legislature to provide for Free Schools. *(margin note)*

5. The Legislature shall provide for the support of free schools, by appropriating thereto the interest of the invested "School Fund", the net proceeds of all forfeitures and fines accruing to this State under the laws thereof; the State capitation tax; and by general taxation of persons and property, or otherwise. It shall also provide for raising, in each county or district, by the authority of the people thereof, such a proportion of the amount required for the support of Free Schools therein as shall be prescribed by general laws.

6. The school districts into which any county is now divided shall continue until changed in pursuance of law.

Levies to be reported to Clerk of County Court. *(margin note)*

7. All levies that may be laid by any county or district for the purpose of free schools shall be reported to the Clerk of the County Court, and shall, under such regulations as may be prescribed by law, be collected by the Sheriff, or other collector, who shall make annual settlement with the County Court; which settle

ments shall be made a matter of record by the Clerk thereof, in a book to be kept for that purpose.

8. White and colored persons shall not be taught in the same school.

9. No person connected with the free school system of the State, or with any educational institution of any name or grade, under State control, shall be interested in the sale, proceeds or profits of any book or other thing used, or to be used therein, under such penalties as may be prescribed by law; *Provided,* That nothing herein shall be construed to apply to any work written or thing invented by such person. *School officers not to be interested in sale of books*

10. No independent Free School district, or organization shall hereafter be created, except with the consent of the school district or districts out of which the same is to be created, expressed by a majority of the voters voting on the question. *Independent Districts.*

11. No appropriation shall hereafter be made to any State Normal School, or branch thereof, except to those already established, and in operation, or now chartered. *Normal Schools.*

12. The Legislature shall foster and encourage moral, intellectual, scientific and agricultural improvement; it shall, whenever it may be practicable, make suitable provision for the blind, mute and insane, and for the organization of such institutions of learning as the best interests of general education in the State may demand. *Legislature to encourage improvements.*

THE SCHOOL LAW.

CHAPTER XLV.

Of Education.

School districts.

1. Every magisterial district in each of the counties of the State shall be a school district, and the same shall be divided into such number of sub-districts as may be necessary for the convenience of the free schools therein. The present districts and sub-districts shall remain until changed in the manner prescribed by law.

Election of County Superintendent. Term of office.

2. A county superintendent of free schools in each county shall be elected by the voters thereof, at the general election held on the Tuesday after the first Monday in November, 1894, and every four years thereafter, whose term of office shall commence on the first day of July next after his election and continue for four years and until his successor shall be elected and qualified according to law.

Election of President and commissioners. Term of office.

There shall also be elected at said election, in each district of the county, by the voters thereof, and every four years thereafter, a president of the board of education, whose term of office shall commence on the first day of July next after his election, and continue for four years, and until his successor is elected and qualified according to law. There shall also be elected at the same time in each district in the county by the voters thereof, one commissioner at the general election held on the Tuesday after the first Monday in November, 1894, a successor to the commissioner elected in May, 1891, and every two years thereafter one commissioner, whose term of office shall commence on the first day of July next after their election, and continue for four years, and until their successors are elected and qualified according to law.

Board of education; who constitute.

The said president and commissioners shall constitute the board of education in the district in which they are elected. No person shall be eligible to more than one office under the provisions of this chapter at the same time. The county superintendent of free schools shall, immediately upon receiving the certificate of election from the commissioners of the county court, forward a written notice thereof to the State Superintendent of Free Schools.

In case of a tie in the vote for members of the board of education, the county superintendent of free schools shall give the casting vote; and in case of a tie in the vote for a county superintendent of free schools, the presidents of the several boards of education in the county shall, at a meeting called for that purpose, at the court house of the county, by the clerk of the county court, not less than six nor more than twelve days after the result of such election is ascertained, appoint one of the persons receiving the highest number of votes for said office, at the said election, as county superintendent of free schools, who shall give notice as aforesaid to the State Superintendent of his appointment. A notice of such meeting shall be made out by the clerk of the county court, and served upon each president of the board of education in the county at least three days before the day of such meeting, by the sheriff, or other officer, to whom the same may be delivered to be served. *Tie vote; how decided.*

The ballots used at said election shall also have written or printed thereon the words, "For school levy", or "Against school levy", as the voter may choose, and the boards of ballot commissioners in the several counties of this State shall have printed at the bottom of each ticket on the official ballot in seperate lines the words "For school levy", and "Against school levy"; and upon the application of the board of education of any district they shall also have printed on said ballots the words, "For —— months school", and "Against —— months school", as provided in this chapter. *Levy.* *Increase in length of school term.*

If a majority of the ballots cast upon the question of laying the school levy in a district, have written or printed thereon, "For school levy", it shall be the duty of the board of education to make the levies required by the 38th and 40th sections of this chapter, annually, for the next four years; but if a majority of the ballots cast in a district have written or printed thereon, "Against school levy", no levy shall be made by said board for the year next succeeding. But it shall be the duty of said board to cause a special election to be held on the Tuesday after the first Monday in November, next thereafter, at which the question of levy, or no levy, shall in like manner be again submitted to the people for their decision, and if a majority of the ballots cast at such special election be, "For school levy", such levy shall be made as hereinbefore required. *Special election; for what purpose; when.*

Of every such special election the secretary of the board of education of the district shall give notice, by *Secretary to give notice of election.*

posting the same at each place of voting in the district
at least ten days before the day on which the same is to
be held. The election to be held on the third Tuesday
in May, 1893, for the purpose of electing county superintendents of free schools in the different counties of
this State, and members of the various boards of education, shall be held according to law; but their terms of
office shall expire as soon as their successors are elected
and qalified, at the election to be held on the first Tuesday after the first Monday in November, 1894.

I. A person elected to any office, whether State, county or district, must
be a resident of the political division to which his powers and duties are
limited. (See Code, chap. vii. sec. 8.)

Commis-
sioner of
election.

3. Any person who may act as commissioner of any
election, held under any of the provisions of this chapter, who shall wilfully reject the vote of any person entitled to vote at said election, or receive the vote of any
person not so entitled, or who shall knowingly make
any false return of the result of any such election, or of
any poll held at any place of voting, shall be guilty of
a misdemeanor, and fined not less than fifty dollars, and
imprisoned not less than twenty days.

Trustees;
appointment
of

4. At the meeting of the district board of education,
held on the first Monday in July, 1881, they shall appoint three intelligent and discreet persons, as trustees
for each sub-district in their district, one of whom shall
be appointed for one year, one for two years, and one
for three years; and the board of education shall thereafter annually appoint one trustee, who shall hold his
office for three years; and the said trustees shall hold
their respective offices until their successors are appointed and qualified.

Vacancies,

5. Vacancies in the office of school trustee shall be
filled by the board of education for the unexpired term;
and in the board of education, by the county superintendent of free schools, for the unexpired term.

II. The appointment of a person to fill a vacancy of president of the board
of education makes such person president of the board.

III. Vacancy in the office of county superintendent is filled by the presidents of the boards of education.

IV. Section 3 of Article XII. of the Constitution provides that the Legislature may provide for county superintendents and other school officers
and defines their duties, powers and compensation. Section 6 of chapter
45 delegates to the county superintendent the power to fill vacancies in the
board of education for the unexpired term. I do not think section 7 of
Article IV. of the Constitution or sections 8, 9 or 10 of chapter 4 of the Code
control as to apportionment of members of boards of education. I am,
therefore, of the opinion that persons appointed by the county superintendent to fill vacancies in the board of education hold for the unexpired
term.—T. S. Riley, Attorney-General.

5*a*. Every school trustee, and every president *Time in which* and commissioner of the board of education elected *to qualify.* within this State shall, within ten days after his election has been duly declared, qualify as such by taking and subscribing, before some one duly authorized to administer oaths, within his county, the oath of office prescribed by section five of article four of the Constitution, which oath shall be filed with the secretary of the board of education of his district.

6. The boards of education of the several districts *Boards of* shall hold their first meeting for each school year on the *first meeting.* first Monday in July. At this meeting they shall determine the number of teachers that may be employed in the several sub-districts and fix the salaries that shall be paid to the teachers. In determining the salaries, they shall have regard to the grade of teachers' certificates, fixing to each grade the salary that shall be paid to teachers of said grade in the several sub-districts, as follows: Teachers having certificates of the grade of number one, shall be paid not less than twenty-five dollars per month; those holding certificates of the grade of number two, not less than twenty-two dollars per month; and those holding certificates of the grade of number three, not less than eighteen dollars per month. And the trustees of the several sub-districts shall in no case transcend or diminish the salaries so fixed in any contract they may make with teachers.

A quorum of the board of education shall consist of *Quorum.* a majority of the members thereof, and in the absence of the president one of said members may act as such; but they shall do no official business except when assembled as a board, and by due notice to all the members, except that the president and secretary may sign orders upon the sheriff for any sum of money which may have been already ordered to be paid.

The members of the board of education shall receive *ompensa-* as compensation for his services the sum of one dollar *on.* and fifty cents per day, to be paid in like manner as the salary of the clerks of the boards of education; *Provided*, That no member shall receive pay for more than six days' services in any one year.

V. A board of education has no authority to annul a teacher's certificate for any cause. Only the county board of examiners can do this.

VI. Boards of education fix the term of school for the whole district.

VII. If a sub-district for any cause fail to have a school in any year it can not have a longer term than the other schools of the district in the following year.

VIII. It is the duty of the county superintendent to issue orders for the pay of members of the board of education. If satisfied the service has been rendered, but this should not be done before the first day of June of each year.

IX. Members of boards of education of independent districts, where not otherwise specially provided, are entitled to pay as provided in the general school law.

X. If officers of town corporations also act as the school board for the independent district, they are entitled to the same pay as district school officers of the same grade; *Provided*, they receive no compensation from the town corporation for their services.

XI. Only one payment of $1.50 per day, for not exceeding six days can be made for services of any member of a board of education, and the successor gets nothing if the predecessor received pay for the six days allowed.— *Alfred Caldwell, Attorney-General.*

XII. The board have the power to fix the salary to be paid teachers as a class based upon the grade of the certificate they hold, but in my opinion they can not require the trustees to employ a teacher of a certain grade. The trustees have the unquestioned right to employ a teacher of any grade certificate which entitled him or her to teach, and pay the salary fixed by the board for that grade.— *T. S. Riley, Attorney-General.*

Board of Education a Corporation.

7. The board of education of each district and independent school district shall be a corporation by the name of "The board of education of the district or independent school district of ————, in the county of ————", and as such may sue and be sued, plead and be impleaded; and as such corporation, shall succeed and be substituted to all the rights of the former township and district boards of education; and may prosecute and maintain any and all suits and proceedings now pending, or which might have been brought and prosecuted in the name of any such former board of education for the recovery of any money or property, or damage to any property due to or vested in such former board.

The said board shall also be liable in its corporate capacity for all claims legally existing against the board of education of which it is successor. Said board shall receive, hold and dispose of according to the rules of law and the intent of the instrument conferring title, any gift, grant, devise or bequest, made for the use of any free school or schools under their jurisdiction; and without any transfer or conveyance, shall be deemed the owner of the real and personal property of their district, and the property of the former township or district for which their district was substituted.

Process on board; how served.

Process and notice may be served on said corporations by delivering a copy thereof to the secretary, or any two members of the board. And all suits or proceedings now pending in any of the courts of the State, in the name of the board of education of any district for any demand or claim in favor of the board of education of any township or district, are hereby made valid.

8. The board of education, at their first meeting after their election, shall appoint a secretary, who shall not be a member of the board, and who shall attend all meetings of the board, and record their official proceedings in a book kept for that purpose, which record shall be attested by his signature and the signature of the president of the board, and which shall, at all reasonable times, be open to the inspection of any person interested therein; he shall have the care and custody of all papers belonging to the board containing evidence of title, contracts or obligations, or being otherwise valuable, and preserve the same in his office, properly arranged for reference, and shall record and keep on file in his office such papers and documents as the board or the law may direct.

Secretary of the Board of Education.

He shall keep such accounts and prepare and certify such reports and writings pertaining to the business of the board, as the board or law may direct. He shall publish within three days after any meeting of the board of education an abstract of the proceedings thereof, by posting the same at the front door of the place of meeting. He shall within ten days after the annual levy is laid certify to the county superintendent of free schools, the total value of all property, real and personal, in his district, with rate of levy, and amount thereof, keeping separate the rates and amounts of teachers' and building funds; and said superintendent shall within twenty days certify the same to the State Superintendent of Free Schools, using blanks therefor, furnished by said State Superintendent. He shall also have authority to administer oaths to school officers in all cases where they are required to take an oath as such.

Secretary; reports of.

For his services as secretary he shall receive such compensation as the board may determine from year to year, not to exceed fifteen dollars, to be paid out of the building fund by an order drawn by the county superintendent, when after an examination by said superintendent of said secretary's books, they are found to be correct. But such order shall not be drawn until the secretary shall have made his annual report to the county superintendent as hereinafter provided, and be approved by the said county superintendent. (See also Sec. 21.)

Secretary; compensation of.

XIII. Teachers are school officers.

XIV. The office of secretary of the board of education is held at the will of the board. The secretary may be relieved at any time by the board.

XV Secretaries of boards of education make but one report per year to the county superintendent. The two blanks are sent to each secretary that he may retain a copy of his report in his office. Special information must be furnished by the secretary to the county superintendent at any time required.

14 SCHOOL LAW OF WEST VIRGINIA.

XVI. The secretary's annual report cannot be completed before the sheriff's settlement with the board of education. County superintendents are forbidden by law to issue orders for the pay of secretaries until they present correct and complete reports.

XVII. The law does not specify who shall call the meetings of the board. The board should adopt a rule upon this subject at its first meeting in the school year, when all its members are present.

Board of Education; powers and duties of.

9. The boards of education shall have general control and supervision of the schools and school interests of their districts; they may determine the number and location of the schools to be taught; change the boundaries of their sub-districts, and increase and diminish the number thereof, having due regard for the school houses already built, or sites procured, assigning, if practicable, to each sub-district not less than forty youths between the ages of six and twenty-one years; *Provided,* That every village consisting of fifty inhabitants or more, shall be included in one sub-district. *And*

Change in sub-district.

provided, further, That no change in any sub-district shall take effect, except immediately after the annual apportionment of the general school fund. When such village as is mentioned in this section is divided by district or county lines, the said village shall be included in the sub-district, to be under the supervision of the board of education of the district to which the largest division of its territory is attached, and said board shall define and enter of record in the office of their secretary the several district and sub-district lines.

Appeal to County Superintendent.

Any person aggrieved by any decision of the board of education, changing the boundaries of a sub-district, or increasing or diminishing the number of the sub-districts, in their district, under this section, may appeal therefrom to the county superintendent of schools, and have the same corrected, if erroneous. Every such person shall present to the county superintendent his petition, signed by himself and at least five other residents of the sub-district, stating the action of the board complained of, and the grounds of appeal; and the county superintendent shall thereupon fix a time and place for the hearing of the appeal, and cause a notice thereof to be served upon the president or the secretary of the board of education, at least five days before the hearing. If, upon hearing the proofs and allegations of the parties, the superintendent be of the opinion that the action of the board complained of was illegal or improper, he shall reverse or correct the same; otherwise the said action shall be affirmed.

XVIII. Where the county court of a county changes the boundary lines of a district or increases or diminishes the number of districts after the annual levy has been laid for school purposes, and the salaries of teachers fixed in the respective districts, and provides that such change or changes shall take effect before the end of the school year (June 30), the schools and school officers should continue as if no change had been made, making settlements, &c., until the close of the year, when the changes ordered should be recognized.

XIX. The building of school houses is discretionary with the boards of education. There is no power in any other court, body or person to compel them to build a school house.—*Alfred Caldwell, Attorney-General.*

XX. The appeal to the county superintendent under this section is *limited* to cases involving the changing of boundaries of a sub-district, or increasing or diminishing the number of sub-districts.

10. The board of education shall cause to be kept in Schools must be provided. every sub-district of their district, by a teacher or teachers of competent ability, temperate habits and good morals, a sufficient number of primary schools for the instruction of the persons entitled to attend the same, and should the trustees of any sub-district neglect or fail to employ a teacher for their sub-district, upon complaint thereof, it shall be the duty of the board of education to do so.

The following persons when residing in a sub-district, Who may attend school. with intent to make such sub-district their home, shall have a right to attend and receive instruction at the primary schools thereof, that is to say: Every youth between the ages of six and twenty-one years, shall have such right; and any other person wishing to receive instruction at any free school in this State, shall have a right, with the assent of the trustees, to attend such school, and the teacher or teachers there employed shall give instruction to such person the same as is required by law for other persons, upon the payment of tuition Who to pay, tuition. fees, not to exceed one dollar and fifty cents per month for each pupil, and upon such other terms as the trustees of the sub-district may prescribe. Said tuition fees shall be paid in advance to the sheriff, who shall give his receipt therefor, and place the amount to the credit of the teachers' fund of said district.

10*a*. Every person having under his control a child Compulsory Attendance. or children between the ages of eight and fourteen years, shall cause such child or children to attend some public school in the city, independent district, or district in which he resides, and such attendance shall continue for at least sixteen weeks of the school year, provided the school be in session as many as sixteen weeks, and for every neglect of such duty the person offending shall be guilty of a misdemeanor, and shall upon conviction thereof before any justice be fined two dollars for the first offense, and five dollars for each subsequent offense. An offense, as understood in this act, shall consist in failure to send to school any child or children for five consecutive days, except in case of the sickness of such child or children or other reasonable excuse.

Trustee and
teacher to
inform.

And it shall be the duty of every trustee and teacher to inform against any one so offending and upon a failure so to do they shall be guilty of a misdemeanor, and be fined not exceeding five dollars; [*Provided,* That if such child or children have attended for a like period of time a private day school, or if such child or children have been otherwise instructed for a like period of time in the branches of learning required by law to be taught in the public schools, or have already acquired such branches, or if his physical or mental condition is such as to render such attendance inexpedient, or impracticable, such penalty shall not be incurred;] *Provided,* further, That in case there be no public school in session within two miles by the nearest traveled road, of any person in the school district, he shall not be liable to the provisions of this act.

Any fines so collected shall be placed to the credit of the building fund of the district.

If sixty per cent. of the legal voters of any city, independent district, or sub-district shall petition the board of education against the enforcement of this act, the said act, so far as that sub-district is concerned, shall be null and void until the beginning of the next school year.

Justices of the peace shall have jurisdiction in all violations of this act in their respective counties.

XXI. A teacher has no authority to admit or exclude pupils from a school, whether from the same or another sub-district, without the consent and direction of the trustees of the school. This does not refer to his right to suspend a pupil for disorderly conduct.

XXII. The teacher has no right to receive the tuition of pay pupils and have it deducted from his month's salary when his order is drawn.

Branches to
be taught.

11. In the primary schools there shall be taught orthography, reading, penmanship, arithmetic, English grammer, physiology, general, United States and State history, general and State geography, single entry book-keeping, civil government, and in addition thereto the theory and art of teaching. It shall be the duty of the State Superintendent to prescribe a manual and graded course of primary instruction to be followed in the country and village schools throughout the State, arranging the order in which the several branches shall be taken up and studied, and the time to be devoted to them, respectively, with provisions for advancement from class to class, also for the examination and graduation of all pupils who satisfactorily complete the prescribed course.

XXIII. A board of education has no authority to prescribe additional branches to those provided by law, or to require them to be taught.

XXXI. The Theory and Art of Teaching as enumerated in Section 11, is not to be understood as being one of the branches required to be taught in the primary schools, but teachers are required to pass an examination in the same,—See Section 29,—as they are in all branches required to be taught under the provisions of this section.

XXXII. Trustees should be very careful not to unnecessarily interfere with a teacher in relation to matters pertaining to the conduct and government of his school. I do not think a teacher should be compelled to give instruction to pupils * * in all branches prescribed by law without reference to proper grade.—*Alfred Caldwell, Attorney-General.*

XXXIII. It is the official duty of the county superintendent to see that the graded course of study for country and village schools is thoroughly introduced into the said schools of his county. But it is not the county superintendent alone upon whom this responsibility rests. The law makes it the duty of members and secretaries of boards of education and of trustees and teachers as well, to perform their whole duty, seeing to it that the course of study, with grading according to accompanying plan, shall be fully introduced into every country and village school in the State.

11a. I. That the nature of alcoholic drinks and narcotics, and special instruction as to their effects upon the human system, in connection with the several divisions of the subject of physiology and hygiene, shall be included in the branches of study taught in the common or public schools, and shall be taught as thoroughly and in the same manner as other like required branches are in said schools, and to all pupils in all said schools throughout the State. *Nature and effects of alcoholic drinks must be taught.*

II. It shall be the duty of the proper officer in control of any school described in the foregoing section to enforce the provisions of this act; and any such officer, school director, committee, superintendent or teacher who shall refuse or neglect to comply with the requirements of this act, or shall neglect or fail to make proper provisions for the instruction required and in the manner specified by the first section of this act, for all pupils in each and every school under his jurisdiction, shall be removed from office, and the vacancy filled as in other cases. *Fine for failure to teach.*

III. No certificate shall be granted to any person to teach in the public schools of the State, after the first of January, anno domini, eighteen hundred and eighty-nine, who has not passed a satisfactory examination in physiology and hygiene, with special reference to the nature and the effects of alcoholic drinks and narcotics upon the human system. *Teachers to be examined.*

12. The trustees shall be under the supervision and control of the board of education, and in all cases the action of the trustees shall be subject to the revision and correction of the board of education, on the motion *Trustees under control of the board.*

of any member thereof, or upon the complaint in writing of any three tax-payers of their sub-district.

Transfer of pupils.

Whenever it shall happen that the persons authorized to attend school are so situated as to be better accommodated at the primary school of an adjoining sub-district, whether in the same or in an adjoining district or county, or whenever it may be necessary to establish a school composed of pupils from parts of two sub-districts, whether in the same or in an adjoining district or county, it shall be the duty of the trustees of the sub-districts interested to transfer such persons for school purposes to the sub-district in which such school house is, or may be, situated; but the enumeration of youth shall be taken in each sub-district as if no transfer had been made, and the trustees of the sub-district in which the school is situated shall have the management of such school.

Tuition.

But in all cases of transfer of pupils from one district to another, the board of education of the district from which the transfer is made shall pay to the board of education of the district in which the school is carried on, such proportion of the cost of said school, as the scholars so transferred bear to the whole number of scholars taught in such school.

XXXIV. "This section was not intended nor does it authorize trustees to transfer pupils from a sub-district to an independent school district."— *Alfred Caldwell, Attorney General.*

XXXV. The cost of the tuition of the transferred pupils should be estimated from the time the transfer takes effect until it expires or the pupils are withdrawn.

XXXVI. No transfer is complete until the trustees of the sub-district to which transfers have been made have agreed to accept the pupils.

XXXVII. When pupils are transferred to an adjoining sub-district in another district it is the duty of the trustees making the transfers, although they are not required to do so by statute, to notify their board of education of all transfers made by them, and the said board of education is required by this section to pay to the board of education of the district to which the pupils have been transferred such proportion of the cost of said school or schools as the pupils so transferred bear to the whole number of pupils taught in said schools during the time of the transfers.

Time of electing teachers.

13. The trustees of every sub-district shall have charge of the schools therein and shall meet at the school house of their sub-district on the third Monday in July of every year, or as soon thereafter as practicable and appoint a teacher or teachers for the coming session of their school, and in such appointment at least two of the trustees, who are the trustees for the ensuing year, shall concur, and such appointment shall be in writing in the form of a contract, according to the form furnished by the State Superintendent of Free Schools and said form shall state that the trustees whose signatures are affixed thereto, met together as herein re-

Form of contract.

quired, and said contract shall be filed with the secretary of the board before the beginning of the term for which said teacher is employed.

If the appointment of any teacher be otherwise than at a meeting herein authorized, the board of education may declare such contract illegal, if the declaration be made by the board before the time mentioned in the contract for the beginning of the school term. Any teacher so appointed may be removed by the trustees or by the board of education for incompetency, neglect of duty, intemperance, profanity, cruelty, or immorality. *Teacher may be removed.*

The trustees shall exclude from any school under their charge any person having a contagious or infectious disease, and they may suspend or expel any scholar found guilty of any disorderly, refractory, indecent, or immoral conduct, and may refuse to admit such scholar again to the school until satisfied that he will properly conduct himself thereafter. But the trustees shall take no action or proceeding relating to the removal of teachers or the suspension or expulsion of any scholar from school unless at a meeting of which the trustees have all had notice, and when at least two of their number shall be present and concur in such action or proceeding, and their action in each particular shall be subject to the revision and correction of the board of education upon complaint in writing of a majority of the patrons of the school, residing within the sub-district in which such action has been taken. Any trustee may, for good cause shown be removed from office by the board of education upon five days notice in writing, of the cause alleged for his removal, and of the time and place the board will take action thereon. *Pupil may be suspended or expelled.* *Trustee may be removed.*

Whenever at the end of any school month the daily average attendance for that month has been less than thirty-five per cent. of the whole number of pupils enumerated in the sub-districts, the trustees may dismiss the teacher and discontinue the school, unless otherwise directed by the board of education; and no high school shall be continued if at the end of any school month, it has not had an average daily attendance of twenty-five scholars. *Schools may be discontinued.*

And it is further expressly provided that should any trustee of any sub-district or member of the board of education receive any money or other thing of value for his aid, assistance or vote in securing to any teacher a school or employment in any district or independent school district in the State, in which said trustee or member of the board of education is authorized by law to act, shall be guilty of a felony and upon conviction thereof shall be punished as provided in chapter 147 of *Bribery of trustees.*

the Code of this State, and the teacher who offers or ten
ders to such trustee or member of the board of education
any money or other thing of value to influence the same,
in aid of securing a school, he shall be liable to punishment as provided in said chapter.

XXXVIII. Neither boards of education nor trustees have authority to
employ a person to teach in the free schools of this State unless such person presents a certificate in duplicate still in force of his qualification to
teach a school of the grade for which he applies. For decision regarding
duplicate certifiate, see same under section 28. Teachers employed as
substitutes should hold same grade of certificate as those whose places
they fill.

XXXXIX. A teacher has the right to punish pupils placed under his
charge for infractions of the rules governing the school. But like the
parent who has the right to enforce obedience, he is answerable for the
abuse of the trust.

XL. The trustees of a school have authority to contract with a teacher
for the length of time and the price per month prescribed by the board of
education, and the board must provide for its payment.

Trustees shall visit and inspect schools. 14. The trustees shall visit every school under their
charge within two weeks after the opening, and again
within two weeks before the close thereof, and at such
other times as in their opinion may be useful to do so.
During such visits, they shall inspect the register of
every teacher and see whether it has been properly kept,
and ascertain whether the scholars have supplied themselves with books and other things requisite for their
studies, whether the school house and grounds, furniture, apparatus and library are kept in good order;
whether anything injurious to the health is suf-
ered to remain about the house or grounds, and
whether the school house is well ventilated and
kept comfortable, as the season may require; and where
it is necessary, provide and promptly apply the proper
remedy.

They shall also during such visits make such examination and enquiry as they may deem useful respecting the
studies, discipline and general condition of the school,
and the conduct and proficiency of the scholars; and give
such directions or make such suggestions to the teachers,
as in their opinion, will promote the interest of the
school, and the health, morals and progress of the
scholars.

XLI. The duty of visiting the schools is made obligatory upon the trustees, and they should faithfully comply with the law in this matter.

XLII. The leading object of the trustees on this, their first visit, should
be the examination of the sanitary condition of the school building and
out-houses. The health of both teachers and pupils depend upon health-
ful surroundings.

Trustees must keep school house in order. 15. They shall cause the school houses under their
charge and everything pertaining thereto, to be kept in

good order and repair, and for this purpose it shall, among other things, be their duty to cause proper suits and prosecutions to be instituted, in the name of the board of education of the district or otherwise, against every person who shall injure or destroy any school property of which the said trustees have charge; and they shall not, without the permission of the district board of education, allow said school houses to be used for any other purpose whatever, except for the purpose of holding religious or literary meetings and Sunday schools, equally by the various religious denominations that may apply for the same, and further for such other meetings as may be considered beneficial to the public generally under such regulations as to the care thereof as may be prescribed by them; *Provided*, That such meetings shall not interfere with the public schools. Trustees may allow school house to be used for certain purposes.

The trustees shall furnish to the board of education estimates of all improvements necessary to the preservation or repair of buildings, grounds and furniture under their charge.

XLIII. The trustees of a school may allow religious exercises held in their school house. They may prescribe conditions, etc. They may refuse to allow the school house to be used for this purpose. In either case, on motion of any member of the board of education, or the petition in writing of three tax-payers of the sub-district, the action of the trustees may be reviewed and reversed or affirmed. The county superintendent has no authority in the matter.

XLIV. "Debating societies," teachers' meetings, school exhibitions and spelling-schools, together with any other meetings, having for their object the advancement of the school interests of the sub-district, and being of a literary character, if conducted in a respectable manner, come within the meaning of the words "literary meetings," as used in the fifteenth section of the school law.

XLV If the trustees of a school refuse the use of a school house for religious purposes, an appeal may be taken to the board of education. The decision of the board is final, either for or against. They may absolutely exclude all denominations from the school house.

XLVI. Religious and literary societies and teachers of select schools, may be required to give security for the protection of school property where trustees are asked to allow the school house to be used for the meetings of such societies. The use of public school property for such purposes is a privilege, not a right.

XLVII I think that the trustees, with the consent of the board of education, can allow the school house to be used for the purpose of holding a select school; provided it does not interfere with the public school. I am also of the opinion that the action of the trustees in either refusing or granting the use of a school house for the purposes above mentioned may be reviewed by the board of education of the district. The party so occupying the school house may be required to give security for the proper care and use of the building.—*T. S. Riley, Attorney General.*

15*a*. [Section 19, chapter 14*a* code, chapter 13, Acts 1887.] If a person willfully interrupt, molest or disturb any free school, or other school, literary society or any other society formed for intellectual, social or moral improvement, organized or carried on under or in pursuance of the laws of this State, or any Sunday Penalty for interrupting or disturbing school.

school, or other school, or school exhibition, or any society lawfully carried on, he shall be guil'y of a misdemeanor, and fined not less than ten nor more than fifty dollars, or at the discretion of the court, be confined in the jail of the county not more than thirty days, in addition to said fine.

15*b.* If any person shall willfully disturb, molest, or interrupt any literary society, school, or society formed for intellectual improvement or any other school or society organized under the laws of this State, or any school, society, or meeting formed or convened for improvement in music, either vocal or instrumental, or for any moral and social amusement, the person so offending shall be deemed guilty of a misdemeanor, and on conviction thereof, shall be fined not less than five dollars, and may be imprisoned in the county jail not exceeding ten days.

Trustees must keep an account of expenses. 16. The trustees of each sub-district shall keep exact account of all necessary expenses incurred by them in the performance of their duties, and render to the secretary of the board of education, at or before their last meeting for the current school year, written accounts, by items, of all such expenses, which, if the board find correct, they shall pay by an order to the sheriff, drawn on the building fund of the district, signed by the secretary and president.

Trustees may purchase certain articles and make certain repairs. The trustees of any sub-district may purchase fuel, water buckets, brooms, coal hods, shovels, pokers, stove pipes, crayons, erasers and dippers, for use in school rooms. They may make such repairs in windows, doors, benches, desks, floors, walls, ceilings and roofs as will render the house comfortable. For such purchase or repairs they shall render to the secretary of the board of education an account, which, if the board find correct, they shall pay out of the building fund of the district.

Trustees; quorum of No one trustee shall, by himself, have any power to perform any duty required by law of the trustees, who shall meet at a time and place fixed by two of their number, the other having had reasonable notice of such meeting, and two of the trustees shall constitute a quorum, and they shall keep a record of their acts and proceedings in a book to be furnished them by the board of education for that purpose, such book to be turned over by them to their successors in office.

Record of meeting.

XLVIII. While trustees are *appointed by the board of education*, their powers are prescribed and their duties imposed by law; and by section 12. of chapter 45, of the Code, the actions of such trustees are subject to the revision and correction of the board of education on proper motion or complaint made; yet no power is given the board to interfere with or prevent a proper discharge by the trustees, of the duties imposed upon them, as such, by law.

By section 16 of chapter 45 of the Code, it is provided, among other things, that "the trustees of any sub-district may purchase fuel, water buckets, brooms, coal hods, shovels, pokers, stove pipes and dippers for use in school rooms. * * * For such purchases they shall render to the secretary of the board of education an account which, if the board find correct, they shall pay out of the building fund of the district."

If then the board, upon examination or revisal, find the account correct, they cannot alter, amend or repudiate it; but in the language of the law, they shall pay it out of the building fund of the district.—*C. C. Watts, Attorney-General.*

17. White and colored persons shall not be taught in the same school; but to afford to colored children the benefits of a free school education, it shall be the duty of the trustees of every sub-district to establish therein, one or more primary schools, for colored persons between the ages of six and twenty-one years, whenever the number of such persons residing therein, and between the ages aforesaid, exceeds fifteen according to the enumeration made for school purposes. The trustees of two or more sub-districts, whether in the same or adjoining districts or counties, may, by agreement with each other, join in establishing a primary school for colored children residing in said sub-districts, and such schools so established shall be subject to the same regulations as are provided for the schools for white children, in section 12 of this chapter.

White and colored pupils must not attend same school.

XLIX. If the colored population of school age exceeds fifteen, a school *must* be established for their accommodation. If there are not so many, that is if the number be fewer than fifteen, they may be transferred to an adjoining sub-district in which a colored school exists, such transfers to be made according to regulations prescribed in section 12.

L. "When a school has been established for colored pupils under section 17 it must be kept open and continued as long as the schools for whites in the same district. The colored children, after the school is established under that section, are entitled of right to the same apparatus, necessary furniture, and school appliances as well as the same length of school term as the whites in schools of like grade, no matter how little or how great the taxes collected from the colored people of the district may be. There is nothing in the 18th section to affect this view. The 18th section deals with another case entirely and cannot affect in any way a sub-district where a colored school is established in accordance with law."—*Alfred Caldwell, Attorney-General*

18. Whenever, in any school district, the benefit of a free school education is not secured to the colored children residing therein, in the manner mentioned in the preceding section, the fund applicable to the support of free schools in such sub-district, whether received from the State or local taxation, shall be divided by the board of education in the proportion which the number of colored children bears to the number of white children therein, according to the latest enumeration made for school purposes; and the share of the former shall be

Division of funds for benefit of colored children.

set apart for the education of colored persons of the proper age, residing in such sub-district, or district, and be applied for that purpose from time to time in such way as the board of education of the district may deem best. Any board of education failing to comply with this section may be compelled to do so by the circuit court of the county, by *mandamus*.

Enumeration of youth.

19. The board of education of each district and independent school district shall require the teacher or teachers in each sub-district or independent school district, annually, before the close of the school or schools, not later than the first day of April, to make an enumeration of all the youths resident in such sub-district or independent school district, who shall be over six years and under twenty-one years old, on the first day of July following, distinguishing between male and female, white and colored.

The enumeration shall be taken in two classes as follows: One class shall contain all youths between the ages of six and sixteen years, and the other, youths between sixteen and twenty-one years respectively. The enumeration shall be verified by the affidavit of the teacher who took the same, before some person qualified to administer oaths, to the effect that he used all

Enumeration; penalty for not taking.

means in his power to make it, and believes it to be correct, and shall return such enumeration to the secretary of the board of education of the district with the term report of such school, or not later than the first day of April; and unless such enumeration be properly taken and returned, the teacher shall not be entitled to demand payment of the balance due on his salary, or so much thereof as shall be necessary to defray the expenses of the enumeration as herein provided.

Teachers exempt from certain duties.

No teacher in this State shall be required to serve on any jury, nor to work on the roads, while his school is in actual operation.

Enumeration; Secretary to keep record of.

The secretary of the board of education shall keep a record in his office of the enumeration of youth so taken, and shall annually, on or before the fifteenth day of April transmit a certified copy of such enumeration to the county superintendent of his county. When such enumeration for any district or sub-district shall not be received by the county superintendent before the twentieth day of April in any year, it shall be his duty, without delay, to employ a competent person to take and verify the same as aforesaid. The person taking and verifying such enumeration shall be paid a reasonable compensation, to be allowed by the board of education, not to exceed two dollars per day for the time necessarily consumed, and paid by an order of said board, signed by the president and secretary, out of the building fund of such district.

In either case the county superintendent as soon as he County Superintendent receives the enumeration for any district or independent to report. school district, and not later than the first day of May, shall forward to the State Superintendent of Free Schools a statement of the number of youths of school age therein. The State Superintendent of Free Schools shall prescribe and furnish all blanks to be used for taking the enumeration of youth.

LI. A correct enumeration of the school youth is one of the most important matters connected with the school work of the State, for it is the basis upon which the distributable school fund of the State is disbursed. The secretary should carefully examine the enumeration report from every sub-district and satisfy himself of its accuracy.

LII. The secretary of the board is authorized to administer oaths to teachers as to the correctness of their reports of enumeration. See Section 8.

20. The trustees of each sub-district shall make a Trustees report to the secretary of the board of education of their report. district, at or before their last meeting in each school year, setting forth in reference to their sub-district, the following particulars; that is to say: The condition of school houses under their charge; the value and kind of apparatus; the number of volumes in school libraries and their value, with such explanations, remarks and additional information as the said trustees may deem useful, or as the blanks furnished by the State Superintendent of Free Schools may require. They shall also report the same particulars in relation to any schools under their charge for colored persons.

LIII. Trustees should make their annual report as prescribed in form No. 7, at the close of the year (June 30) whether the school closed then or not.

21. The secretary of the board of education to whom Secretary's the report of the trustees shall have been made, as report. provided in the twentieth section, shall revise the said reports, and if they be found erroneous or defective, may return them for correction. From the corrected report and the teachers' registers, provided for in the thirtieth section of this chapter, and such other authentic information as he may be able to obtain, he shall make a report to the county superintendent on or before the twentieth day of July, annually, in tabular form, by sub-districts, embracing each particular reported to him by the said trustees' reports and teachers' registers, and showing the aggregate or average of each, as the case may require, for his district.

Additional report.

And he shall further report to the county superintend- ent on or before the twentieth day of July, annually, the following additional particulars in reference to his district, for the year ending on the preceding thirtieth day of June, that is to say: The rate and amount of the tax levied for the teachers' fund and the building fund respectively; the amount of such taxes collected and placed to the credit of each of these funds; the amount received from the State for the teachers' fund; the amount of the balance in the treasury at the beginning of the school year for each fund; the amount of receipts from all other sources placed to the credit of each fund; the amount expended for the pay of teachers, male and female, white and colored, respectively; the amount of commission paid to the sheriff or collector; the amount of the delinquent list returned by said collector; the amount of the balance in hand at the close of the school year for each fund; the amount expended for the purchase of sites for school houses, and for the construction and furnishing of the same; and for the rent, hire and repair of such property; the amount expended for such furniture, for apparatus, for interest, for the enumeration of youth, and for contingencies; also. the number of volumes in school libraries and their value; total receipts; total expenditures, with such explanations, remarks and additional information as he may deem proper, or as the blanks furnished by the State Superintendent may require. He shall also, in like manner, report all particulars pertaining to any colored school or schools in his district, including the number taught therein, and for what length of time.

Secretary's remuneration for making report.

For this report the secretary shall be allowed out of the building fund, in addition to his salary as secretary, ten dollars; but the board of education shall in no case order this sum to be paid until the county superintendent has certified to them that the said report has been made, and that it is correct and complete, and made within the time specified in this section.

LIV. In the case of summer schools where a part of the term is finished in one year and a part in the next, the financial condition of the district must be reported, just as it is, without regard to what may or may not be contracted for. In the estimate for the levy the amount of partially executed contracts and the balance on hand to pay them must be considered. The statistical report of such schools should be made in the year in which they close.

LV. The secretary's annual report cannot be completed before the sheriff's settlement with the board of education. County superintendents must not issue orders for the pay of secretaries until they present correct and complete reports. The law provides this in declaratory terms.

LVI. Chapter 29, § 67 Code, requires the secretary of every school district and independent school district through which a railroad runs in each county, within thirty days after the levy is laid for free school and building purposes, or either, to certify to the auditor the amount so levied, etc

22. The county superintendent shall receive and revise the reports made to him as aforesaid, and see that they are in proper form and according to intent of law; and when deficiencies or errors are found to exist, shall return them for correction. From these reports and such other authentic information as he can obtain, he shall make report to the State Superintendent of Free Schools, on or before the first day of August, annually, or as soon thereafter as possible, setting forth in reference to each district of his county, for the year ending on the preceding thirtieth day of June, the several particulars mentioned in the twentieth and twenty-first sections, with the proper aggregate or average of each for the county; and shall make the apportionment, and report such apportionment to the auditor, and also report whether the districts have made the levy for school purposes required by this chapter.

County Superintendent's report.

LVII. The report of the county superintendent should be made not later than the first day of August, as prescribed by law, that the State Superintendent may complete his annual report, which he should have compiled for the Governor not later than the first day of October.

LVIII. The apportionment of the General School Fund, made by the county superintendent, should be reported to the State Superintendent, as well as to the auditor.

23. The school year shall commence on the first day of July, and close on the thirtieth day of June, and all reports, accounts and settlements respecting the free schools of this State shall be made with reference to the school year.

School year.

LIX. If any school opens after the first day of April, (the time required for the enumeration to be returned by the teacher), if the teacher so opening the school has not taken the enumeration and returned it, it is the duty of the county superintendent to employ some one, as the law directs, to take the enumeration of that sub-district. The pay to such person would not be properly deducted from the teacher's salary, who opened the school after the time required for the enumeration to be returned.

LX. If a school opens so near the close of the school year that by continuing in session all the school days to the end of the year the term will not be finished before the year closes, the remaining time, under the contract, may be completed in the new year. (In this case the school should be reported in the new year.) If the school open in ample time to finish before the close of the year, but suspends before the term is out, the time can not be added to the next year's term.

LXI. The school law contemplates that the financial affairs shall be closed up at the end of each year.

24. When the board of education of any district deem it expedient to establish a high school, they shall submit the question to the voters of the district on the day and month of election named in section two of this chapter, of any year, in the manner following, that is to say: The board shall prepare and sign a notice setting forth the kind of school proposed; the place where it is to be

High School; mode of establishing.

located; the estimated expense of establishing the same, including cost of site, building, furniture, books and apparatus and the estimated annual expense of supporting the school after it is in operation, with such other information concerning it as they may deem proper; and stating that the question of authorizing the establishment of such school will be submitted to the voters of the district, at the election specified in the notice, which they shall cause to be posted four weeks before the election in at least three of the most public places in the district. A poll shall thereupon be taken upon the said question, at the election specified in the notice, and the result ascertained in like manner as is prescribed in section two of this chapter. The ballots used on voting on the question shall have written or printed thereon the words, "For the high school," or "Against the high school." If it appear by the result of said poll that not less than three-fifths of the voters who voted on the question are in favor of authorizing the establishment of said school, the board of education may then proceed to obtain the site and provide proper buildings, fixtures and improvements, and procure necessary furniture, books and apparatus for the said school, to support the same after it is put in operation; for which pur-

Additional levy for high schools. pose the board may annually levy an additional tax on the property taxable in their district, not to exceed in any one year thirty cents on every one hundred dollars valuation thereof, according to the latest assessment for State and county taxation. The said school shall be under the care and direction of the board of education of the district in which it is established.

LXII. The maximum rate of levy is 50 cents on the one hundred dollars, for country and village schools except as provided in section 40, but for the support of high schools established in accordance with the provisions of this section, there may be an additional levy of 30 cents on the one hundred dollars, thus making the maximum rate for the support of these schools 80 cents on the one hundred dollars, and the power to levy to this extent is granted to the board by the vote of the people when the high school is established.

High school may be established by two or more districts. 25. In like manner, if the boards of education of two or more districts, whether in the same or different counties, deem it expedient to jointly establish and support a high school, they may submit the question of authorizing the same to the voters of their districts, separately, and in the manner prescribed in section twenty-four of this chapter, specifying in the notice the amount or proportion of the expenses which each district is to contribute; and if authorized by not less than three-fifths of the voters voting on the question in each district, may proceed jointly to establish and support the said school; and for that purpose the said boards may annually levy a tax on the property taxable in their respective districts, not to exceed in any one year the rate of thirty cents on every one hundred dollars valuation thereof.

The said school shall be under the care and direction of directors, to be selected and removed from time to time in such manner as the boards of education concerned may agree upon, or when there is no such agreement, under the care and direction of the board of education of the district in which the school house is situated, and the boards of education concerned shall from time to time prescribe such regulations as they may deem necessary respecting the school. *Directors of joint high school.*

26. The board of directors who have the care and direction of the said school shall appoint, and may remove the teachers, shall fix their salaries; prescribe the branches of learning to be taught; the time the school shall be kept open; the ages and qualifications of the scholars to be admitted, admit scholars from non-contributing districts on such terms of tuition as they may deem proper; expel or suspend scholars when necessary; ascertain and certify the expenses of the school, of which they shall cause exact accounts to be kept; and prescribe all needful regulations respecting the school, subject, nevertheless, to any regulations respecting the same that may be prescribed pursuant to the preceding section. *Care and direction of joint school.*

They shall annually report through their secretary on or before the twentieth day of July, to the superintendent of free schools for the county in which the school house is situated, such particulars respecting the schools as the State Superintendent of Free Schools may require; and the county superintendent shall transmit the report, with such remarks and additional information as he deems proper, to the State Superintendent. *Directors' report.*

The boards of education of any district may also establish graded schools in towns, villages and densely populated neighborhoods of their respective districts, employ teachers therefor, and make such special regulations as may be necessary to conduct them. But in every such case involving additional taxation, the matter shall be first submitted to a vote of the people and their consent obtained, as is prescribed in section twenty-four in case of a high school; *Provided*, That no additional levy for a graded school shall exceed in any one year fifteen cents on every hundred dollars valuation. *Provided further*, When any sub-district having graded schools, desire a longer term of school than four months, it shall be the duty of the board of education on the pe- *Graded schools. Levy for graded school.*

tition of the taxpayers of such sub-district to submit the question to the voters of said sub-district, at such time and place as they may fix, by posting notices ten days before said election, setting forth the number of months the said school shall be run, including the State Fund and their proper share of any district levy that may be levied in the districts for the support of the schools of said districts.

Assessor must furnish list of property. It shall be the duty of the assessor, with the assistance of the secretary of the board of education, to furnish such board a list of the property, both real and personal, assessed by him in said sub-district, for State and county purposes. And the said board of education may provide for the extending of the said tax, and provide for the collection of the same, under such rules and regulations as they may provide, and use the fund thus collected for the running of such graded schools.

LXIII. "No vote of the people is necessary as a condition precedent to the establishing of a graded school in a district in case such school does not increase the levy over the fifty cent limit named in section 40 The vote to authorize any levy must be taken as required by section 2 Section 26 specifically requires a vote where the cost involves a levy in excess of such fifty cents. I find no authority for continuing a graded school any longer period than other schools of a d strict."—*Alfred Caldwell, Attorney General.*

LXIV. The number of tax-payers who are to petition for more than five months' school in a sub-district is left to the discretion of the board. There should be a sufficient number on the petition to indicate that the desire was seriously entertained and entitled to respect.

LXV. The vote should be taken not later than the 10th of May, so that if the increased rate of levy is authorized, the assessor may have the necessary time in which to extend same on his books. The rate of levy being 50 cents on the one hundred dollars, the increase to be voted upon can not exceed fifteen cents additional, making the maximum levy for the support of a graded school 65 cents on the one hundred dollars.

LXVI. "The board should have the sheriff collect the taxes for the graded school. They should enter an order authorizing him to collect. It would not be best to order the collection by any one else."—*Alfred Caldwell, Attorney-General.*

County board of examiners. 27. There shall be in every county, for the purpose of examining and certifying teachers, a county board of examiners, to be composed of the county superintendent, who shall be *ex-officio* president, and two experienced teachers, each of whom shall have received a teacher's state certificate or a number one county certificate, or be a graduate of some reputable school, to be nominated by the county superintendent and appointed by the presidents of the district boards of education, at a meeting for that purpose, to be held at the county seat on the first Wednesday in July, 1893, one of whom shall be appointed for a term of two years and one for one year, and thereafter one member annually for a term of two years, at which meeting a majority of said presidents, or any three thereof, shall constitute a quorum. It shall be the duty of the county superintendent to attend such meetings.

Vacancies in said board of examiners shall be filled by the presidents in the same manner as members of said board are appointed, and it shall be the duty of the county superintendent, upon ten days' notice, to call meetings of said presidents at the county seat for that purpose. The board of examiners shall each receive a compensation of three dollars per day for each day actually and necessarily employed in conducting the examinations, and for one day at each of the two stated examinations required in section twenty-eight of this chapter to be spent in consultation and preparation for their duties. This compensation shall be paid out of the fees received from the teachers examined, and shall in no case exceed the amount thereof.

The county superintendent shall collect from every person who applies for examination a fee therefor of one dollar, out of which he shall pay the per diem of the board of examiners, and the expense of the notice required by the twenty-eighth section of this chapter, and the balance, if any, he shall pay to the sheriff, to be placed to the credit of the distributable fund of the county received from the State, and distributed with it. He shall at the end of each school year, make and return to the clerk of the county court, and also to the State Superintendent, a detailed and certified account of the names of all applicants for examination; the amount of the fees received by him for the same; the amount paid out to the members of the board of examiners, and the balance, if any, placed to the credit of the distributable fund of the county as aforesaid.

Vacancies.

Compensation of examiners.

County Superintendent to collect fees and return account.

LXVII. Presidents of independent school districts should participate in the election of members of the board of examiners except where their teachers are not required to be examined by said board, as in Wheeling, Huntington, Charleston, Martinsburg, &c.

LXVIII. No more than two names should be proposed to the presidents of the boards of education at one time for members of the board of examiners. If either or both are rejected, then other nominations should be made.

LXIX. No person other than a teacher should be appointed a member of the board of examiners.

LXX. All appointees must hold No. 1 certificates or their equivalents.

LXXI. The county superintendent has the sole right to name candidates to the presidents for members of the board of examiners.

LXXII. All school officers, including members of the boards of examiners, are required to take the oath prescribed by the constitution, section 5, Article IV.

LXXIII. The presidents of the boards of education have no authority to elect persons members of the board of examiners not nominated by the county superintendent.

LXXIV. The offices of president of board of education and member of the board of examiners are incompatible.

LXXV. In case there is more money received from fees in one examination than pays the per diem of the members of the board and the publication of notice, the residue may be used to pay per diem of members of the board in subsequent examinations in the same year where the receipts are insufficient.

LXXVI. Boards of examiners have the right to limit the time to be occupied by the teachers in answering the questions of each branch.

LXXVII. It is 'the duty of the county superintendent to preserve the manuscripts of the teachers who are examined, for at least one year from their date.

LXXVIII. "It is a gross violation of official duty for the presidents to remain absent from the meeting for the purpose of avoiding the appointment of examiners. They are subject to be fined under § 59 School Law. Examiners hold over until a new appointment is made of successors."—*Alfred Caldwell, Attorney-General.*

Teacher must have a certificate.

28. No teacher shall be employed to teach any public school of this State until he shall have presented to the trustees, directors or board having charge of such school, a certificate in duplicate of his qualifications to teach a school of the grade for which he applies, the duplicate of which shall be filed with the secretary of the board of education of the district in which the school is situated and so endorsed on the original by the secretary; and no salary shall be paid to any teacher unless duplicate be filed as aforesaid.

Teachers examined in certain branches.

The board of examiners shall examine each candidate for the profession of teacher, who may apply to them, as to his or her competency to teach orthography, reading, penmanship, arithmetic, English grammar, geography, history, single entry book-keeping and civil government, if the application be for a primary school, and if the application be for a higher school, they shall examine the applicant as to his competency to teach the additional branches required for such school, and if satisfied of the competency of the applicant to teach and govern such schools, and that he or she is of good moral character and not addicted to drunkenness, they shall give a certificate in duplicate accordingly. The county superintendent shall keep a register of all certificates awarded by the board of examiners, stating the character and grade of certificate and the time when issued.

Certificate in force in county where issued.

No certificate shall be issued by the board of examiners, except upon an actual examination, participated in by a majority of the board, or be of force except in the county in which it was issued, nor for a longer period than one year, except as provided in section twenty-nine of this chapter, and the board of examiners may, upon proper evidence of the fact, revoke the certificate of any teacher within the county, for any cause which would have justified the withholding thereof, when the same was granted, by giving ten days' notice to the teacher of their intent to do so.

The board of examiners shall, at two stated periods in each year, agreed upon by themselves, of which they shall give due notice, hold public examinations, at which all applicants for certificates shall be required to attend; and should circumstances require it, the county superintendent may call extra meetings for the same purpose. County superintendents and members of the board of examiners may be employed to teach without the certificate required of other teachers. But should any member of the board of education or school trustee be employed as teacher, it shall vacate his office.

Examinations held at certain times.

Examiners and superintendent may teach without certificate.

LXXIX. No person shall be employed to teach a public school who has not a teacher's certificate regularly issued and still in force. Substitute teachers are permissible when the teacher is unavoidably absent, and then only, with the consent of the school trustees. Substitutes should have certificates of same grade as those whose places they fill. It is not necessary for the trustees to make a contract with a substitute. A teacher can not engage a school, make a contract for it, then employ a substitute and himself take another school.

LXXX. If a teacher obtain two certificates, the same year, he may contract with the trustees on either, whether of the same or different grades.

LXXXI. The right of a member of the board of examiners to teach without examination is confined to the county in which such position is held.

LXXXII. The board of examiners are required to hold two stated public examinations and, should circumstances require it, extra meetings may be held for the same purpose.

LXXXIII. The members of the board of examiners are authorized to teach without certificates, and are therefore prohibited from issuing certificates to each other.

LXXXIV. Section 30 of chapter 45 of the Code, provides that all certificates for the school year, must be issued after July first, and for that reason the certificate in question would expire with the old school year. * * * There is no provision made for the examination of a county superintendent while in office as he has the right to teach during his term of office without a certificate—*T. S. Riley, Attorney-General.*

LXXXV. The latter part of section 28 of chapter 45 of the Code, provides that there shall be two public examinations at which all applicants for certificates shall be required to attend, and should circumstances require it, the county superintendent may call extra meetings for the purpose. Now, if the certificate granted was given at one of the above meetings, it would be good until the time for which it was given expires * * * I take it that all certificates, except those granted under section 29, expire with the school year. Section 30 provides that no examinations shall be held or certificate granted until after the first day of July of the school year in which said certificates are to be used—*T. S. Riley, Attorney-General.*

LXXXVI. As the law now stands all grades of certificates may be issued at the same examination. (See latter part of section 29, of school law.) The law provides for two stated examinations and should circumstances require it, the county superintendent may call extra meetings for the same purpose. At any of these examinations all grades of certificates may be issued, but the extra meeting should not be called unless it is absolutely necessary to supply teachers for the current school year. The practice of some county superintendents of calling extra meetings and granting certificates after the schools for the year have closed and when it is not necessary to supply teachers for the school year ending July the first following the examination, is not warranted under the law. Such examinations should not be held until after the first of July or in other words after the beginning of the new year. (See section 30 of the school law.) All No. 1 certificates properly granted expire in three years from the first of July following the date of their issue, and No. 2 certificates in one year from the first of July following the date of their issue, and No. 3 certificates expire on the first of July following the date of their issue.—*T. S. Riley, Attorney-General.*

Regulations for Boards of Examiners

29. The following regulations shall be observed by boards of examiners with regard to examinations and granting teachers' certificates:

First. No applicant shall be admitted to examination unless the board shall have reasonable evidence that he or she is of good moral character and temperate habits, and has attained the age of sixteen years.

Second. No college diploma or certificate of recommendation from the president or faculty of any college or normal school or academy shall be taken to supersede the necessity of examination by the board of examiners, nor shall a certificate be granted to any applicant except after a careful examination upon each branch of study and upon the art of teaching.

Third. Boards of examiners and others herein authorized to confer certificates shall state the teacher's grade of proficiency in each branch in which he is examined.

Fourth. They shall grade the certificate granted according to the following scheme numbering them according to the merit of the applicant from one to three:

First grade certificates.

The first grade certificate shall be issued to all applicants who shall pass an examination in all the branches required to be taught in the primary free schools of the State, and in addition thereto the theory and art of teaching, general history, civil government and book-keeping, and obtain a general average of ninety per cent. on a scale of one hundred per cent. and not less than seventy-five per cent. on any one branch; which certificates shall be valid for a period of four years and shall be re-issued once without examination at the discretion of said board of examiners, provided the holder has taught two years on said certificate.

Second grade.

The second grade certificate shall be issued to all applicants who shall pass an examination upon all the branches required to be taught in the primary free schools and in addition thereto civil government and the theory and art of teaching and obtain a general average of eighty per cent. and not lower than seventy per cent. on any one branch, which shall be valid for a period of two years and be re-issued only upon examination.

Third grade.

The third grade certificate shall be granted to applicants who shall pass a satisfactory examination in the branches required to be taught in the primary free schools, and the theory and art of teaching and obtain a general average of seventy per cent. and not lower than sixty per cent. in any one branch, and be valid for a period of one year and be re-issued only upon examination and then not to the applicant more than twice. All grades of county certificates provided by law shall be granted at the same examination. Failure to attend the teachers' county institute where such attendance may be required of teachers holding any of these grade certificates unless excused by law or unless said failure may be for reasons deemed sufficient by the county board of examiners shall be cause for revoking said certificate.

LXXXVII. There is now no distinction made between applicants for certificates. They must all pass examination in all the branches required to be taught in the primary schools of the State and in addition thereto in the theory and art of teaching. See section 11.

29a. I. There shall be a State board of examiners State Board of which shall consist of four competent persons, one from Examiners. each congressional district, to be appointed by the State Superintendent of Free Schools; the term of office of such examiners shall be four years and vacancies in said board shall be filled by the State Superintendent of Free Schools. Said board shall meet at two different places, Meetings. at least, in each congressional district in each year, for the purpose of making the examinations and granting the certificates provided for in this act, and any three of said members shall constitute a quorum.

II. The board thus constituted may issue two grades Grades of of certificates to such as are found to possess the requi- certificates. site scholarship, and who exhibit satisfactory evidence of good moral character and of professional experience and ability, as follows: First class certificates for twelve years; second class, for six years. Any person holding a certificate of the first class, who shall have taught for eight years of said twelve years, shall be entitled, without examination, to have the same renewed at the expiration of the said twelve.

The second class to be issued to applicants of satisfactory attainments in the branches required for county certificates, and in addition, not fewer than four other branches to be determined upon by the board.

The second class certificates shall be issued upon ap- Certificates plication, without examination, to the graduates of the issued to grad-uates of State University of West Virginia, of the Peabody Nor- certain mal College of Tennessee, of the State normal school institutions. and its branches of West Virginia, and of other schools in this State whose grade of work is equal in all respects, in the judgment of the board, to the State normal school and its branches, where graduates shall have presented to the board satisfactory evidence that they have taught successfully three years in the State under a number one county certificate, two of which said three years shall immediately precede the application for such certificate.

First class given on expiration of second.

Teachers who shall present to the board satisfactory evidence that they have taught successfully four years, under a second-class certificate, shall be entitled to receive, without examination, a first-class certificate at the expiration of the second class.

Record.

The board shall keep a record of the proceedings, showing the number, date and duration of each certificate, to whom granted, and for what branches of study, and shall report such statistics to the State Superintendent annually on or before the thirtieth day of September.

Certifiate valid in any school district.

III. All certificates issued by such board shall be countersigned by the Superintendent of free schools; and such certificates shall supersede any and all other examinations of the persons holding them, by any board of examiners, and shall be equivalent to a number one certificate granted by a county board of examiners, and shall be valid in any school district in the State, unless revoked by the State board for a good cause.

Fee.

IV. Each applicant for a certificate shall pay the board of examiners a fee of five dollars.

Compensation of examiners.

V. The board of examiners shall each receive a compensation of five dollars per day actually and necessarily spent in conducting the examinations, and for one day to be spent in consultation and in preparing for their duties, and six cents per mile for each mile necessarily traveled in going to and returning from the place of examination. This compensation shall be paid out of the fees received from the teachers examined, and shall in no case exceed the amount so received.

Annual report to State Superintendent.

Said board shall, at the end of each school year, make and return to the State Superintendent of Free Schools, a detailed and certified account of the names of all the applicants for examination, the amount of the fees received, the amount paid out to the members of the board, and the balance, if any, shall be paid over to the treasurer of the State, to be placed to the credit of the distributable school fund.

LXXXVIII. Graduates of the State Normal School and of the State University, in order to secure the second class certificate, must present to the State board of examiners satisfactory evidence that they have taught successfully three years under a Number 1 county certificate: two of which said years must immediately precede the application for the certificate.

Teachers shall keep daily and term registers.

30. Every teacher shall keep a daily register, and make monthly reports to the secretary of the board of education of his district. He shall also keep a term register, in which shall be entered the date of the commencement and termination of every term of the school;

the name and age of every scholar who attended the
school during said term; the daily attendance, distinguishing between males and females; the branches
taught, and the number of scholars engaged in each
month in the study of each branch, and such other particulars as are necessary to enable the secretaries of the
boards of education, or directors, to make the reports
required of them. The State Superintendent of free
schools shall prescribe such form and regulations, respecting the register to be kept and reports to be made
by the teachers, as shall seem to him necessary.

At the close of each term the register thereof shall be *Penalty for failure to return term register.*
returned by the teacher to the office of the secretary of
the board of education for the district, who shall file the
same and unless such register be properly kept and
returned, the teacher shall not be entitled to demand
payment of the balance due on his salary.

Teachers shall be paid monthly, and by orders on the *Teachers to be paid monthly.*
sheriff or collector, signed by the secretary and president
of the board, which said orders when signed as aforesaid and delivered to the teacher shall be deemed at once
due and payable. Where any teacher has taught according to his contract, for one month, the trustees for the
sub-district in which he has so taught, shall certify the
fact to the secretary of the district board, whereupon
he shall receive from said secretary an order upon the
sheriff or collector of the county, signed by the secretary
and president of the board of education for one month's
salary; but in no case shall such order be given, unless
the monthly report containing the facts required in the
preceding part of this section, to be shown in the term
register, be first duly made out and returned to the
secretary.

The school month shall consist of twenty days, exclud- *School month.*
ing Saturdays, all of which shall be devoted to teaching
the school contracted for.

As a means of improving the teachers, and fitting *Teachers' institutes.*
them for more effective service in the free schools of the
State, teacher's institutes shall be held annually throughout the State, one or more in each county; they shall be
held at such times and places as the State Superintendent
shall, with the advice of the county superintendent,
direct, and shall continue each for one week of five days;
they shall be conducted by experienced and skillful
institute instructors, who shall be appointed by the State
Superintendent, but it shall be a part of the duty of the
county superintendent, under the instructions of the
State Superintendent, to make all proper arrangements
for the institutes, and to assist in conducting them.

Instructors' compensation. The instructors whom the State Superintendent shall employ, as herein provided, shall each receive for his services not more than twenty-five dollars for each institute he may instruct, to be paid out of the general school fund, on a proper order of the State Superintendent, but the aggregate amount of such compensation for the whole State shall not exceed one thousand dollars.

Examination. At the close of the institutes, as herein provided, and during the week following, the county board of examiners shall hold one of the two examinations prescribed in section twenty-eight: *Provided*, That no examination shall be held or certificate granted until after the first day of the school year in which said certificates are to be used.

Graded course of institute work. It shall be the duty of the State Superintendent to prescribe a graded course of institute work covering a period of two years, and the methods of conducting the same, together with such other details connected therewith as he shall deem conducive to their usefulness and efficiency.

Graded course of professional study. It shall also be the duty of the State Superintendent to prescribe a graded course of professional study covering a period of two years, which shall embrace history of education, school management, methods of teaching and educational psychology. **Who exempt from institute attendance.** Any teacher who has completed the graded course of institute work and the graded course of professional study, and passed a satisfactory examination thereon, and also obtained a number one teacher's certificate, shall be exempt from further compulsory institute attendance.

Failure or refusal to attend institute. Any teacher not exempt from institute attendance who shall fail or refuse to attend at least one institute annually, held under the provisions of this section, unless such teacher shall have an excuse therefor, sufficient in the judgment of the board of examiners to which such teacher may apply for examination, shall not be entitled to examination or be employed to teach any free school during the year within which such failure or refusal may have occurred.

LXXXIX. The secretary of the board should carefully examine the monthly summary which the teacher files at the end of each month, for it should contain a summary of what the teacher is recording in his term register, which is to become the chief basis of the secretary's report to the county superintendent. In no instance should the secretary issue the teacher's order for his last month's salary until the term register is found to contain all data required by the above section, to be recorded in it.

XCI. "The applicant for examination for a teacher's certificate must have attended one institute during the year or have an excuse for not so attending sufficient in the judgment of the board of examiners to entitle such applicant to be examined. Such attendance within the year, or such excuse is a condition precedent to the right to be examined."—*Alfred Caldwell, Attorney General.*

XCI. When only a few days of a school term run into a new year the school may be reported in the old year, but if a month or more of the school runs into the new year, then it should all be reported in that year.

XCII. The per cent of attendance and absence should make 100 without the per cent. of non-membership.

XCIII. In making reports to the secretary, teachers should not count children of the sub district not enrolled in the school—when a child is once enrolled he should be accounted for during the whole term, both be· fore and after he is enrolled.

XCIV. It is the duty of the presidents and secretaries of the boards of education to issue orders for money directed to be paid by the board.

XCV. The following excuses are deemed of sufficient importance in all departments of life and may be regarded good for non-attendance at the institute: Sickness, death of a near relative, and attendance at court under summons. Frivolous and petty excuses should not be accepted.

XCVI. "The trustees, if they employ a teacher who has not complied with the law requiring teachers to attend institutes, violate their oath of office, and ought themselves to be removed if it is done wilfully."—*Alfred Caldwell, Attorney-General.*

XCVII. The holding of an examination or the issuing of a certificate in any year prior to the first day of July is prohibited by law, The school year begins with that date, and all certificates should be issued with reference to it. If a certificate—good for one year, be issued in the autumn or later, it terminates with the first day of the ensuing July, and so with a two or four years' certificate issued at the same time would end with the first day of July two or four years hence.

31. In contracts with teachers, it shall be understood Holidays. that school is not to be kept in operation for ordinary instruction on the first day of January, fourth day of July, or the twenty-fifth day of December, nor any National or State festival or Thanksgiving day; but the month or time mentioned in such contract shall nevertheless be computed as if the said days were included.

XCVIII. The day of election is not a national or State festival or thanksgiving day and does not come under the provisions of section 31 of charter 45 of the Code, and therefore teachers are not entitled to credit for this day.—*T. S. Riley, Attorney-General*

XCIX. I think from a liberal construction of section 31 that it is intended that in months in which there is a holiday the number of days actually taught is one less than the number required by law for months in which there is no holiday. In taking this view I think the teacher would be entitled to credit for Christmas, but not for the day previous on which the school was not in session.—*T. S. Riley, Attorney-General.*

32. All teachers, boards of education, and other school Teaching officers are hereby charged with the duty of providing morals. that moral training for the youth of this State which will contribute to securing good behavior and manners, and furnish the State with exemplary citizens. It shall Building fires. also be the duty of every school trustee to see that the school house is kept clean and in good order, and that fires, when necessary, are made and kept therein, but no expense shall be incurred therefor, to exceed fifty cents per week, and the amount thus expended shall be certified by the trustees to the board of education, and shall,

if correct, be paid out of the building fund of the district.

C. I am of opinion, that under the foregoing provision, trustees have the power to incur the expenses therein provided for, and that where it is necessary, in order to comply with the requirements of said provision, they not only have the power, but it is their imperative duty to incur the expense necessary to that end—not exceeding fifty cents per week. I am further of opinion that, upon a proper certificate of the expenditure of such amount being furnished the board of education of the district in which such expenditure is made, it will be the duty of said board to provide for the payment of the same out of the building fund of the district, provided, of course, *the account is correct.*

The board of education can make no order by which this power or duty can be taken from the trustees. The law on this subject is explicit, and contemplates a specific compliance therewith.

There is no conflict between the above quoted provisions and others of chapter 45. The board of education have the "power of revisal and correction" as to *this* provision, to the extent of seeing that the amount expended *is correct,* but not to the extent of nullifying a plain provision of law—*C. C. Watts, Attorney-General.*

CI. Persons building fires should have a definite contract with the trustees.   *   *   *   *   *   *   *   *   *

"The Legislature intended by enacting § 32 to compel the trustees to have school houses kept clean. fires made and kept, &c., by expenditures out of the building fund.   *   *   *   *   *   *   *

The trustees have no right to alter the form of appointment prescribed by the State Superintendent so as to make it a duty of the teacher to do this work for the salary he is to get out of the 'teacher's fund.'   *   *   I fully concur with the opinion given by my predecessor (General Watts) upon the section named."—*Alfred Caldwell, Attorney-General.*

President of Board shall examine all school houses

33. The president of the board of education of every district shall, at least once a year, examine the school houses and school house sites in the district, and report the condition of the same to the board; and such as are, in their judgment, properly located and are sufficient, or can with reasonable expense be rendered so, shall be retained for the use of public schools, and the remainder, with the consent of the county superintendent,

School buildings may be sold.

shall be sold at public auction or otherwise, by the board of education, and on such terms of sale as the board may order and the proceeds added to the building fund: *Provided,* That the grantor or his heirs of any such school house site shall, if he or they so desire, have the same reconveyed to him or them, without the buildings thereon, (if any), upon paying to the board of education the amount received by such grantor for such site; or in case no compensation was paid therefor, the same shall be so reconveyed free of charge. In case of such reconveyance, the building on such site (if any) shall be sold, as hereinafter provided, with privilege to the purchaser to remove it from off such site in a reasonable time. This proviso shall not be construed to apply to any school house lot within any village, town or city.

CII. "I am of the opinion that the board has the right to sell the old school house notwithstanding the fact that the legal title had not been conveyed. This was an inadvertance that no one can take the advantage of. The equitable title was in the board. I think the board can sell the house as provided in section 33 of chapter 45 of the Code."—*T. S. Riley, Attorney-General.*

34. The board of education of every district shall The board shall provide suitable houses, grounds, &c. provide by purchase, condemnation, leasing, building or otherwise, suitable school houses and grounds in their districts, in such locations as will best accommodate the inhabitants thereof, and improve such grounds and provide such furniture, fixtures and appliances for the said school houses, as the comfort, health, cleanliness and convenience of the scholars may require, and keep such grounds, school houses, furniture, fixtures and appliances in good order and repair: *Provided*, That in case such boards of education shall be unable to agree upon a proper location for a school house in any sub-district, such location shall be decided by the county superintendent.

Boards of education in adjoining districts or counties Districts may join in erecting school houses. may jointly provide for the erection of school houses for the accommodation of adjoining portions of districts or counties, for high schools, union schools or sub-district schools, which from local causes, can not be conveniently attached to sub-districts in the districts or counties to which they belong. The title to such houses Title to joint building invested in. shall be vested in the board of education having supervision of the sub-district containing the greatest number of children, and terms indicating a trust for the purpose aforesaid shall be introduced into an agreement made between the boards of education interested. Such school houses shall be provided with furniture, fixtures and such other appliances as are supplied to school houses generally. An equitable amount shall be assessed on each district interested, by the respective boards of education, for the purpose aforesaid. Boards of education shall in every case require bond of all contractors, with approved security, in double the amount of the contract for building or repairing school houses.

No county superintendent, board of education, or any Officers not to be personally interested in contract. member thereof, or trustee of any sub-district, shall, directly or indirectly, become personally interested in any contract for building or repairing school houses in his or their district; and any county superintendent, member of such board, or any trustee, violating this section, shall be guilty of a misdemeanor and fined not less than one hundred dollars.

CIII. "The length of a school term in union schools must be determined by the term fixed by the district in which the school is located, for its schools. The trustees of the sub-district of the location of the school would control the school house, &c. All the boards of education of the district out of which the pupils are sent have to do, is to pay a just part of the expense of the union school."—*Alfred Caldwell, Attorney-General.*

CIV. In case the land owner, on whose land a school house is built by a board of education before a deed is delivered therefor, refuses to make the deed, proceedings in a court of equity may be instituted by the board to compel the specific performance of the contract.

CV. Chapter 65, Acts 1879, makes it a misdemeanor for any county or district school officer to become directly or indirectly pecuniarily interested in contracts, lettings and furnishings in cases where he has a voice or control.   See Acts 1879, chapter 65, wherein it is provided that: "It shall be unlawful for any member of a county court, overseer of the poor, district school officer, or any member of any other district board, or for any county or district officer to be or become, directly or indirectly, pecuniarily interested in the proceeds of any contract or service, or in furnishing any supplies in the contract for, or the award or letting of which, as such member or officer, he may have any voice or control."   See also section 13 of this chapter.

CVI. When the board fail to agree upon the location of a school house, and the county superintendent is called to decide the matter, his decision is final, and from it no appeal can be taken.

CVII. A county superintendent has no authority to select a site for a school house. He can only act when the board of education fail to agree as to a location.

Plans must be submitted to County Superintendent. 35. No school house shall be erected unless the plan thereof shall have been submitted to the county superintendent, and approved by him, and it is hereby made his duty to acquaint himself with the principles of school house architecture, and, in all his plans for such structures, to have regard to economy, convenience, health and durability of structure.

CVIII. The approval of the plans of school houses is, perhaps, the most important duty which the county superintendent has to perform. He is thus made the architect of school house construction in his county, and if the same are illy constructed, poorly ventilated, poorly lighted, and improperly heated, thus producing physical injury to the pupils, he is morally responsible.

Land for school site may be condemned. 36. When land has been designated by the board of education of any district as a suitable location for a school house and the necessary buildings, or for enlarging a school house lot, if the owner or owners refuse to sell the same, or demand a price therefor which is deemed by the board unreasonable, or the owner is a *feme covert*, a minor, *non compos mentis*, or non-resident, after ten days' notice, served upon such owner or owners, or the owner or owners being non-residents thereof, by publication for four weeks in some newspaper published in the county, or if there be no newspaper published in the county, by posting the same for four weeks at the front door of the court house, and five other public places in the county, at least two of which shall be in the district and one in the sub-distict in which such property is located, the board may petition the circuit court of such county to have such lots of ground condemned for the use of public schools, and such proceedings shall thereupon be had in the name of such board for the condemnation thereof, as provided for in chapter forty-two of this Code: *Provided*, That the land so taken shall not exceed in quantity one acre.

CIX. When condemnation proceedings become necessary, the board o education should consult and advise with the prosecuting attorney who will instruct it how to proceed according to the provisions of chapter XLII, of the Code of West Virginia.

37. All school houses, school house sites and other property belonging to any board of education and used for school purposes, shall be exempt from execution or other process, and from lien on, or distress for taxes or county levies; but when any order of the board, upon the sheriff of the county, or judgment or decree for a sum of money against the said board has been presented to such sheriff without obtaining payment, payment thereof may be enforced by the circuit court by *mandamus* or an order for specific levy on the property taxable in the district. *School property exempt.*

37*a*. Whereas it is represented to the legislature that, prior to the introduction of the present free school system, many lots or small pieces of land were donated or purchased, and the title thereof, legal or equitable, vested in trustees with the view of erecting thereon buildings designed exclusively for educational purposes, and that they were used for such purposes many years prior to the formation of the State, and are still used or claimed by the boards of education in the various school districts in many of the counties of the State, and that said trustees in many cases have departed this life or left the State, and others since the introduction of the free school system have declined to act or take any interest in, or control over, such lands; therefore,

Be it enacted by the Legislature of West Virginia:

1. That the title of all such lands be, and the same is hereby vested in the board of education of the school district in which such lands as have been in the actual possession of the board of education for the last five years, and are still in such possession and not otherwise claimed, may be, and their successors in office, to be held and used for free school purposes, and none other. *Title to certain lands.*

2. If from any cause the board of education of the school district in which any such land may lie, shall be of opinion that the interest and convenience of the schools of such district will be promoted by the sale of any such lands, they may sell and convey the same, and use the proceeds of such sales in the purchase of other lands and the erection or repair of other buildings to be used and held for free school purposes, as in other cases. *Certain lands may be sold.*

38. To provide school houses and grounds, furniture, fixtures and appliances, and keep the same in good order and repair, to supply said schools with fuel and all other things necessary for their comfort and convenience, and to pay any existing indebtness against the building *Levy for Building Fund.*

fund and all other expenses incurred in the district in connection with the schools, not chargeable to the "teachers' fund," the board of education shall, annually, on the first Monday in July, or as soon as practicable thereafter, levy a tax on the property taxable in each district, not to exceed, in any one year, the rate of forty cents on every hundred dollars valuation thereof, according to the latest assessment on the same for State and county taxation.

CX. The levy for the Building Fund is limited to forty cents on the $100, except in the case of high schools organized under the provisions of section 24 of this chapter wherein it is provided that for the equipment and support of these high schools 30 cents *additional* may be levied, thus making the rates of levy 70 cents on the $100.

CXI. It is the duty of boards of education to levy for a sufficient amount for both teachers' and building funds, to do all that is necessary to have all the schools in their respective districts taught five months in the year unless such amount would require a levy of more than the maximum rate fixed by law. See section 40 and decisions thereunder.

CXII. Power of board to purchase outline maps and dictionaries—"Section 14 seems to imply that there may be apparatus and library connected with a public school   Section 16 limits power of trustees but not the board of education as to expenditures for certain articles. I am inclined to a liberal construction of the law in respect to what is a proper expenditure of the building fund. I believe outline maps, dictionaries for reference and any other necessary apparatus for the instruction of the scholars in the branches to be taught in the school, reasonable in amount, can be purchased out of the building fund at the discretion of the board of education by virtue of the authority conferred by the 34th section upon such board to provide such furniture, fixtures and appliances for the school houses as the convenience of the scholars may require."—*Alfred Caldwell, Attorney-General.*

Building Fund.

39.   The proceeds of taxes so levied, of school houses and sites sold, of all donations, devises and bequests applicable to any of the purposes mentioned in the preceding section, shall constitute a special fund to be called the "building fund," to be appropriated exclusively to the purposes named in the preceding section,

CXIII. A balance due the building fund should not be taken by the board to pay debts against the teachers' fund, nor should money be taken from the teachers' fund to pay claims against the building fund.

CXIV. Insurance paid for the destruction of a school house by fire is paid to the credit of the building fund of the board of education generally, and may be used to erect another building in the same or a different place, or for other purposes, as the board may direct.

CXV. To supersede or correct a school levy by the circuit court. For process, see Acts of 1875, chapter 72, and Wells, *et al vs.* Board of Education, 20 W. Va. 157.

Levy for support of schools

40.   For the support of the primary free schools of their district and in each independent school district, and to pay any existing indebtedness against the "teachers' fund," the board of education thereof shall annually, on the first Monday in July or as soon thereafter as possible levy, by the authority of the people, as prescribed in section two of this chapter, such a tax on the property

taxable in the district as will, with the money received from the State for the support of free schools, be sufficient to keep schools in operation at least five months in the year; *Provided*, The said tax in any one year shall not exceed the rate of fifty cents on every one hundred dollars valuation, according to the latest available assessment made for State and county taxation. The proceeds of this levy, together with the money received from the State as aforesaid, shall constitute a special fund to be called the "teachers' fund," and no part thereof shall be used for any other purpose than the payment of teacher's salaries; first for the current year, and any part of said fund not so expended, shall be appropriated to the payment of any existing indebtedness created for said purpose. Upon the failure of any board of education to lay such levy as is hereby required, or any other levy provided for in this chapter they shall be compelled to do so by the circuit court of the county by a writ of *mandamus*, unless good cause be shown to the contrary.

Limit of levy.

Teachers fund.

Board may be compelled to levy.

But in case the levy provided for in this and the thirty-eighth section of this chapter shall not be sufficient to pay any existing indebtedness of the district, in addition to the other purpose for which it is levied, the board may increase such levy to the amount actually necessary, or lay a special levy for the purpose. And in no case shall the appropropriation of any money to the payment of any existing indebtedness, directly or indirectly, interfere with the payment of teachers' salaries for the term of five months, for which the schools are required by law to be kept open in each year.

Special levy

CXVI. Section 51 of chapter XXXII, of the Code, provides that: "On real and personal property, not exempt from taxation," there shall be collected ten cents on every one hundred dollars' valuation thereof, for the support of free schools. See sections 60 and 61 of this Chapter.

CXVII. Under the provisions of this section, the free schools must be kept in operation at least five months in the year, and as many more as may be determined by the voters of the district.

"In districts in which the fifty cent levy will not be sufficient to maintain the schools for five months, the board of education has the power to increase the levy to the amount actually necessary to make up the deficiency, or they may lay a special levy for that purpose."—*T. S. Riley, Attorney-General.*

CXVIII. A board of education has no authority to close the school of a district before the term of five months, required by law, and contracted to be taught by the teachers, has been finished, on account of lack of funds.

CXIX. A board of education may be compelled by a writ of *mandamus* to levy at a sufficient rate to run the schools of a district five months, if the people have directed by vote that the levy be made and the rate of levy does not exceed the limit prescribed by law which may under the provisions of section 40, by special levy exceed fifty cents on the $100.

CXX. A board of education violates a plain provision of the law when it pays "existing indebtedness" out of the levy for the current year and thereby shortens the term of the schools of the district below five months. A sum necessary to run the schools five months must be provided, and if anything is left it may be applied to existing indebtedness.

Longer term than five months.

41. If the board of education of any district agree that the school in their district should be continued more than five months in the year, or if twenty or more voters of the district ask it, in writing, they shall submit the question to the voters thereof at the next general election, which order shall state also the length of time for which it is proposed to continue the schools. Ballots may be used for voting on the question, on which may be written or printed "for —— months schools"; for those who are in favor of more than five months school; those who oppose a longer term than five months may vote with a ballot having written or printed on it, "against more than five months school." And if the proposition for a longer term than five months have a majority of all the votes cast for and against, then the board shall order the levy accordingly. *Provided*, That in any district where a poll is held for a purpose herein specified, notices of such election shall be posted by the secretary of the board of education in at least three public places in the district, at least three weeks before the day of voting; and the notice shall explicitly state the term of time for the school, which is to be voted for, and only two terms of time shall be voted for at any one election. And the time of the term voted for at such election shall continue for two years. The poll shall be held and the election conducted, and the official records returned as prescribed in the second section of this chapter.

The trustees in each sub-district may, in their discretion, order all the schools under their jurisdiction to begin in any month in the school year.

To get share of State fund levy is necessary.

42. No district or independent school district shall hereafter receive any share of the distributable State fund for free schools, in any year in which the levy required by the fortieth section has not been made in such district or independent school district; and any money heretofore or hereafter distributed, and undrawn and remaining credited on the books of the auditor to any such district or independent school district on the thirtieth day of June in each year, shall, on that day, be transferred on the books of the auditor to, and form a part of, the general school fund to be distributed.

CXXI. It is the duty of the county superintendent of any county in which a district or districts have voted down the levy, to inform the Auditor of the same, giving name or names of said district or districts, that he may properly transfer that part of the State fund due such district or districts for that year to the general school fund. See section 61, last clause.

Assessor's certificate basis for school levy.

43. The assessor of every assessment district shall make out and deliver to the secretary of the board of education of each district in his district, on or before the first day of July in each year, a certificate showing

the aggregate value of all personal property; and the clerk of the county court shall certify to the said secretary the aggregate value of all real estate in such district or independent school district, which certificates shall serve as a basis for any levy that may be made for school purposes for that year.

44. Immediately upon the receipts of the certificates mentioned in the preceding section, and of the notice from the county superintendent, as hereinafter provided, showing the amount of the general school fund to which such district, or independent school district, is entitled, it shall be the duty of the board of education of such district, to determine the rates of taxation necessary, for the pay of teachers and for the building fund in their district for the school year, and for the payment of any such existing indebtedness, as aforesaid, and report the same, by their secretary, to the clerk of the county court, to the county superintendent, and also to the assessor; and thereupon, it shall be the duty of the said assessor to extend on his books of assessment for State and county purposes, the amount of taxes levied as aforesaid, in two separate columns, the one headed "teachers' fund," and the other "building fund," from which extension the sheriff shall proceed to collect the same, and shall account therefor as required by law. *Board must determine rate of taxation.*

Any assessor who shall fail to make out and deliver the certificate mentioned in the forty-third section, and any secretary of a board of education who shall fail to make out and deliver the certificate named in this section, shall be fined twenty dollars for the benefit of the building fund of the district. And any assessor who shall charge on the assessor's books, as provided in the preceding section, a greater amount of taxes than is due from the person charged therewith shall, in such case, if the overcharge be inadvertently made, be fined double the amount, and if wilfully made, ten times the amount of the overcharge, one-half thereof to be applied to the benefit of the building fund, and the residue to the informer. *Fine in certain cases.*

The fines provided for in this section may be recovered, on motion of any citizen of the district, or sub-district, in which such overcharge or delinquency of the assessor or secretary shall occur or in which the property overcharged may be, on ten days' notice before any justice of such district, or by indictment in the circuit court. *How fine recovered.*

CXXII. The rate of taxation and levy cannot be determined and laid before the first Monday in July of each year. See form of proceedings at this meeting, in Appendix.

Board must not create debt. 45. It shall not be lawful for the board of education of any district, or independent school district, to contract for, or expend in any year, more than the aggregate amount of its quota of the general school fund, and the amount collected from the district or independent school district levies for that year, together with any balance remaining in the hands of the sheriff, or collector, at the end of the preceding year, and such arrearages of taxes as may be due such district or independent school district.

Debt may be created in certain cases. But in districts wherein there is a town or city with an enumeration of youth of school age of three hundred or over, the board of education of such district may borrow money and issue bonds therefor for the purpose of building, completing, enlarging, repairing or furnishing school houses, in such town or city. Said bonds shall be payable not exceeding ten years from their date, and the rate of interest thereon shall not exceed six per centum per annum, but in no other case shall any debt be incurred by such board to be paid out of school money for any subsequent year: *Provided,* That no debt shall be contracted under this section which shall, including existing indebtedness, in the aggregate, exceed five per centum on the value of the taxable property in said district, to be ascertained by the last assessment for state and county taxes previous to the incurring of such indebtedness, nor without at the same time providing for the collection of a direct annual tax sufficient to pay annually the interest on said debt, and the principal thereof, within and not exceeding thirty-four years; and, *provided, further,* that no debt shall be contracted under this section unless all questions connected with the same shall have been first submitted to a vote of the people of said district, **Issuing bonds, must be voted on by the people.** and have received three-fifths of all the votes cast for and against the same. Such election shall be held and conducted in the same manner as the general school election provided for in this chapter.

If the trustees of any district, or any board of education shall make any agreement for the employment of a teacher in violation of this section, or for any other object concerning free schools under their charge, so as to occasion thereby the aggregate of the just claims **Trustees or Board individually responsible.** against the board of education of the district, or independent school district, in any year, to exceed its aggregate receipts, as aforesaid, for such year, such board of education, or trustees, shall be individually responsible to the teacher, or other person with whom such agreement is made.

The board of education of each district, and independent school district, in each county, shall require its secretary, ten days prior to the first day of July, in each year, to prepare and post at three places of election within said district, or independent school district, and in each school district and independent school district where the expenditures for all school purposes in any one school year in said district shall equal or exceed the sum of three thousand dollars, said board of education shall also publish in some newspaper of the county having a general circulation in the district, an itemized statement, duly sworn to by the president and secretary of said board, showing all moneys disbursed by said president and secretary by orders on the sheriff, or otherwise, within the school year, last preceding, distinguishing between the teachers' fund and building fund. The statement shall give the name of each person to whom an order shall have been issued, and shall state the object for which it was given.

CXXIII. The law maks no provision for additional compensation for the secretary in consideration of making up the statements to be published by boards in all districts having an annual expenditure of $3,000 or more.

CXXIV. An important case arising under the provisions of Section 45, was decided by the Supreme Court of Appeals, December 6, 1893, and is reported in 38 W. Va., p. 382. The syllabus reads as follows:
1. *Schools and Schoolhouses—Boards of Education—Contracts—Construction of Statutes*
Under section 45, c. 45, of the Code, the value of a school house and site yet unsold, though the board of education intends to sell it, can not be taken into consideration in estimating the amount of money available in the fiscal year for contracts and expenditures.
2. *Schools and schoolhouses—Boards of Education—Contracts—Construction of Statutes.*

Where a contract between a board of education and contractors for building a schoolhouse fixes a sum as the contract price, which may exceed the amount of money available under section 45, c. 45 of the Code for a fiscal school year, but contains a provision that no liability shall be imposed by such contract on the board for anything beyond the sum lawfully available under that section, so as to prevent the contractors from recovering of the board anything beyond such sum, the contract is not unlawful under said section, so as to prevent the board from paying upon it such money as is applicable under said section.

46. The sheriff or collector of the county shall receive, collect and disburse all school moneys for the several districts and independent districts therein, both that levied by said district and that distributed thereto by the State. He shall be required by the county court to give in addition to his bond as collector of the State and county taxes a special bond in approved security in a penalty equal to double the amount of school money which will probably come into his hands for school purposes during any one year of his term of office, which shall be made payable to the State of West Virginia, with one or more sureties deemed sufficient by such court, and proved or acknowledged before such court and an order stating such proof or acknowledgment shall be entered of record by such court.

Duties sheriff.

He shall keep his accounts with the several boards of education of each district and independent school district: one of money belonging to the teachers' fund and the other of money belonging to the building fund, and shall credit every receipt and charge every disbursement to the fund to which it belongs. He shall pay out no money standing to the credit of the board of education, except upon an order signed by the secretary and president thereof, specifying the sum to be paid and the fund to which it is to be charged; or upon a certified copy of a judgment, or a decree of a court of justice against the said board, for a sum of money therein specified; or upon an order of the county superintendent, as provided in section eight of this chapter.

Sheriff's settlement with boards.

He shall, on, or immediately before, the first day of July in each year, settle with the board of education of each district and independent school district, in which settlement he shall be charged with the amount of taxes levied by the board of education upon the property of the district or independent school district, for the teachers' fund and building fund, and to pay any indebtedness of the district, and with the amount distributed thereto from the general State fund, and for any other moneys received by him during the current year on account of the free schools of such district or independent school district; and he shall be credited with the amount of delinquent school taxes of such district or independent school district that has been duly returned by him and certified by the clerk of the county court to such board of education.

He shall also be credited in such settlement with all vouchers produced by him, if found to be correct by the district board of education, and he shall receive no other credits except his commission as hereinafter provided; an account of this settlement shall be made out by each board of education, naming the district for which it is made, with the proper debits and credits which were the subjects of this settlement. They shall also number all vouchers with which the sheriff has been credited by them, end endorse on the back of each the words, "Settled by B. E." Under this endorsement the secretary of the board shall sign his name and date of settlement.

Sheriff's settlement with county court.

All such accounts and vouchers so endorsed shall then be delivered to the sheriff or collector whose duty it shall be to deliver them to the clerk of the county court, which accounts and vouchers shall serve as a basis of the settlement to be made by the sheriff or collector, with the county court, according to Article XII. and section 7 of the Constitution, and section fifty-two of this chapter. If any sheriff or collector shall pay out in any one year, more money on account of the teachers' fund or building fund than shall have been levied and could have been collected by him during said year, together with the amount remaining in his hands from any preceding year, he shall in such settlement, receive no credit for such excess.

He shall receive no pay for receiving and disbursing the State school fund, and not more than two per cent. for receiving and disbursing railroad taxes, and no pay for the disbursement of any school money, arising from the sale of school property or received from any other source than levies. If he fail to account for and pay over, as required by law, any money which may come to his hands, or for which he is liable, judgment may be recovered therefor against him and his securities, with interest and ten per cent. damages; and upon the failure of such sheriff to pay any proper draft which may be drawn by the said board of education upon him, the person entitled to receive the sum of money specified in such draft may require the sheriff to endorse thereon, or write across the face thereof the words "presented for payment," with the proper date, and sign the same, and judgment upon motion therefor may be obtained against the sheriff before any justice of his county, or before the circuit court thereof, with interest from the time said draft was presented and ten per cent. damages, he having had at least ten days' notice of the motion: *Provided*, That no sheriff shall be required to endorse any school order, nor shall suit be brought on any such school order prior to the first day of November of the current school year.

[margin notes: Sheriff's commission on railroad taxes. Sheriff to endorse drafts.]

CXXV. Where error is discovered after a settlement has been made it may be corrected by proper legal proceedings.

CXXVI. See Code, chapter 41, section 56, as to penalty for sheriff, who shall fail or refuse to pay any draft or order lawfully drawn upon him, under certain circumstances.

CXXVII. "Neither the board of education as a corporation, nor the members thereof individually, are liable to a sheriff who has paid out more in any year, on account of the teachers' fund, than has been levied and could have been collected by him during such year, together with the amount remaining in his hands from any previous year."—*Alfred Caldwell, Attorney-General.*

CXXVIII. School orders shall be received at par value in payment of taxes, county and district levies, militia fines and officers' fees, etc.—See section 10, chapter 41, Code.

CXXIX. There is no law providing for the payment, by boards of education, or fees to county clerks for preparing abstracts of sheriffs' settlements as required by section 52; or certifying delinquent lists to Boards of education, as required of him by this section, or for certifying the value of real estate to said boards as he is required to do by section 45. This work is a part of his duty as a county officer, for which he is paid a salary out of the county treasury by the county court.

47. The delinquent lists for district levies shall be returned and real estate sold therefor, as hereinafter provided.

Such lists of delinquent lands shall be in form, or in substance, as follows:

"List of real estate in the district of ——, in the county of ——, delinquent for the non-payment of school taxes thereon for the year — —:"

Name of Person.	Estate held.	Quantity of land.	Description and location of land.	Distance and bearing from courthouse.	Teachers' fund.	Building fund.	Special levy.	Why returned delinquent.

The delinquent lists of personal property shall be in form or in substance as follows:

"List of personal property in the district of ——, in the county of ——, delinquent for non-payment of school taxes thereon for the year ——:"

Name of Person.	Total value of Personal property charged.	Teachers' fund.	Building Fund.	Special levy.	Why returned delinquent.			

And the sheriff or collector returning such lists shall, at the foot thereof, subscribe the following oath: "I, A—— B——, sheriff, (deputy sheriff or collector), of the county of ——, do swear that the foregoing list is, I verily believe, correct and just; and that I have received no part of the taxes for which the real estate (or personal property, as the case may be), therein mentioned is returned delinquent, and that I have used due diligence to find property within my county liable to distress for said taxes, but have found none."

48. The said lists shall be returned to the county court, before the first day of July in every year, and a list of real estate shall be examined, corrected and allowed by said court, and a copy thereof certified to the auditor, and another copy to the assessor for future use in making out the next land book. The list of personal property shall also be examined, corrected and allowed by the court, and the amount thereof so allowed, together with the amount allowed of the list of real estate, shall be certified by the clerk of said court, to the secretary of the board of education of the proper district. The original list shall be preserved by the clerk of said court in his office.

Property lists disposition

CXXX. Secretaries should see to it that clerks of the county courts furnish them with these lists before the first Monday in July, as required by law.

49. The auditor shall include the school taxes on real estate so returned delinquent, in his list to be furnished the sheriff for sale for deliquent taxes.

Return of delinquent land.

50. There shall be a lien on all real estate for the district levies assessed thereon, from the day fixed by law for the commencement of the assessment of taxes therein for such year, and interest upon such levies at the rate of six per cent. per annum, from the twentieth day of January in the year following that in which the assessment is made, until payment.

Lien on real estate for levies.

51. A copy of the list of personal property, returned delinquent for the non-payment of district levies, shall be placed by the clerk of the county court in the hands of the sheriff or collector for collection, to be collected and accounted for by him, in the same manner as for levies originally placed in his hands for collection; and he may collect such levies by distress or otherwise, at any time within two years after they are so placed in his hands.

List of personal property returned delinquent.

52. Every sheriff or collector shall be allowed five *per centum* commissions on the collection of all district levies for free school purposes. In addition to the settlements required to be made with each board of a district, every sheriff or collector of school moneys shall also make annual settlements, by districts, with the county court of his county, at its next term after the first day of July of each year, showing the amount of all moneys received and disbursed by him for the preceding year

Sheriff's commission on district taxes.

for school and building purposes from State and from the district and independent school district funds, and the amount due to each district; which settlement shall be made a matter of record by the clerk of said court, in a book to be kept for that purpose. All accounts and vouchers required to be returned to the clerk of the county court by section forty-six of this chapter, shall be filed by said clerk in his office, and the file of each district shall be kept separate.

Penalty for failure to make settlements. If any sheriff or collector of school moneys shall fail to make the settlement required by this section at the time required, without reasonable cause therefor, he shall forfeit fifty dollars to the general school fund, and a like penality shall be incurred by him for each subsequent term of the court that shall pass without such settlement. And the sheriff or collector shall moreover, be charged with twelve per cent. interest on all school moneys in his hands for the time he is in default in making the settlement required in this section, which interest shall be charged up against him when the settlement shall be made.

Prosecuting Attorney shall take action. When the sheriff or collector shall fail to make this settlement at the time required herein, it shall be the duty of the prosecuting attorney to proceed by action against him and his securities in the circuit court, to recover the fine imposed upon him by this section. Every sheriff or collector shall, moreover, be liable to any person injured in consequence of his failure to make the settlement herein required. This settlement shall extend back to the commencement of the term of office of such sheriff or collector.

Members of board fined. If any board of education fail to make the settlements required by section forty-six of this chapter, with the sheriff, when requested by him to do so, each member of such board so failing or refusing shall be fined twenty dollars, for the benefit of the school fund.

The clerk of the county court shall transmit an abstract of the settlement to the State Superintendent of Free Schools within ten days after the same has been made.

And the retiring sheriff shall within sixty days after he shall have made his final settlement in the manner herein provided, pay and turn over to his successors in office such balances as may be shown due from him by said settlements upon such order as is prescribed by section forty-six of this chapter, and if he fail to do so, he shall be liable to the forfeit and penalty herein prescribed.

CXXXI. This abstract of the settlement with the sheriff should be promptly forwarded to the State superintendent, by the county clerk, immediately after the settlement with the sheriff made at the next term of the county court after the first day of July annually, as required by section 52.

53. The county superintendent of schools shall be a person of good moral character, of temperate habits, literary acquirements, and skill and experience in the art of teaching. He shall receive for his services an annual compensation, as follows: In counties having not more than fifty schools, one hundred and fifty dollars; in counties having more than fifty and not more than seventy-five schools, two hundred dollars; in counties having more than seventy-five and not more than one hundred schools, two hundred and fifty dollars, and in counties having more than one hundred schools, three hundred dollars, which salary shall be paid ratably for any shorter term of service than one year. *County Superintendent, qualifications and salary.*

Such compensation shall be paid quarterly, upon orders drawn by the county superintendent on the State Superintendent of Free Schools, who shall, upon receiving the same, draw his warrant upon the auditor therefor, payable to such county superintendent, or to such person as he may direct. But the final payment shall not be made until the county superintendent has made the reports required of him to the State Superintendent of Free Schools. The same shall be paid out of the general school fund, but the amount thereof shall be deducted by the auditor from the amount next to be distributed to each county. *Salary, how paid.*

He shall, before entering upon the duties of his office, execute a bond, conditioned according to law, before the county court of his county, or the clerk thereof in vacation, in the sum of five hundred dollars, with approved security, upon which bond he shall be liable in any court having jurisdiction, to any person or persons, or to any board of education, for losses sustained by reason of his neglect; or non-performance of duties imposed by this chapter. Said bond shall be filed in the office of the clerk of the county court, who shall within five days certify to the State Superintendent of Free Schools the name of said county superintendent and his post office address: *Provided*, That the county superintendents heretofore elected shall continue in office until their successors shall have been elected and qualified under this chapter. *County Superintendent's bond.*

A vacancy in the office of county superintendent shall be filled for the unexpired term by the presidents of the boards of education in the county, at a meeting to be called for that purpose by the clerk of the county court, at the court house of the county, within thirty days after the vacancy occurs. A majority of said presidents *Vacancy, how filled.*

shall be necessary to constitute a quorum at such meeting.

CXXXII. County superintendents must make their reports to the state superintendent full and complete before making requisition for last quarter's salary; and the state superintendent must see to it that said report is full and accurate before issuing his requisition upon the Auditor for said last quarter's salary of county superintendent.

CXXXIII. The offices of county superintendent and of notary public are not incompatible.

CXXXIV. County superintendents have no official authority over the question of the rate of wages to be paid in the several districts. Boards of education fix the rate to be paid each grade, provided that they do not go below $25 per mouth for grade No. 1; $22 for No. 2; and $18 for No. 3 certificates. See section 6.

CXXXV. The county superintendent should not pay the secretaries until he has examined their books and found them correct. If he does this he violates the plain provision of law as set forth in section 8 of this chapter.

CXXXVI. The salary of the county superintendent depends or is regulated by the number of schools, and I have no doubt that if the number of schools increase so as to increase his salary during his term of office he is entitled to such increased salary.—*T. S. Riley, Attorney-General.*

County Superintendent to visit schools.

54. The county superintendent shall visit each school within his county, at least once in each school year, at such time as he may deem necessary and proper, and note the course and method of instruction and the branches taught, and give such directions in the art of teaching, and the method thereof in each school, as to him shall seem necessary or expedient, so that the uniformity in the course of studies and methods of instruction employed shall be secured, as far as practicable, in the schools of the several grades, respectively.

He shall acquaint himself, as far as practicable, with the character and condition of each school, noting any deficiencies that may exist, either in the government of the school, the classification of its scholars, or the method of instruction employed in the several branches, and shall make such suggestions in private to the teacher, orally or by writing, as to him shall appear to be necessary to the good order of the schools and the progress of the scholars- He shall note the character and condition of the school houses, the sufficiency or insufficiency of their furniture and fixtures, and shall make such suggestions to the several boards of education and trustees as in his opinion shall seem conducive to the comfort and progress of the scholars in the several schools.

County and union institutes.

55. It shall be the duty of the county superintendent to aid the teachers in all proper efforts to improve themselves in their profession. For this purpose, he shall encourage the formation of county institutes for mutual improvement; shall attend the meetings of said institutes

whenever practicable, and give such advice and instruction, in regard to their conduct and management, as in his judgment will contribute to their great efficiency. In connection with superintendents of the adjoining counties, each county superintendent shall encourage the formation of union institutes; shall attend and participate in the exercises of the same, as far as practicable; and shall use all proper means to improve the efficiency of the teachers and to elevate their profession.

He shall at all times conform to the instructions of the State Superintendent of Free Schools, as to the matters within the jurisdiction of the said Superintendent, and shall serve as the organ of communication between him and the several district boards of education. He shall distribute from his office all blanks, circulars, copies of school laws and other communications from the State Superintendent to the several boards and persons entitled to receive the same.

56. In addition to the reports mentioned in the twenty-second section, it shall be the duty of the county superintendent to make out and transmit to the State Superintendent of Free Schools a detailed report of the condition and character of the schools within his county, noting all deficiencies and suggesting their remedies, with such remarks upon the operations of the school laws as his experience and observation may suggest, pointing out wherein he considers them deficient. He shall also report such districts as have failed to make returns of the enumeration of youth as required in the nineteenth section of this chapter; and also those districts that have failed to make the levy required in section forty. It shall be the duty of the county superintendent to make in a well bound book to be kept for the purpose, a record of all his proceedings; of all certificates issued by the board of examiners, and of all reports made by him, which book shall be the property of the office; and all outgoing county superintendents shall make the report required for each year of their service. *County Superintendent's reports.*

CXXXVII. The law as laid down in section 56, is explicit in requiring a written report of the condition of the schools and school work over which they have supervision. Blank pages are found in the county superintendent's "annual report" and the same should be properly filled.

57. No school officer, or teacher of any free school, shall act as agent for any author, publisher, bookseller, or other person, to introduce or recommend the use of any book, apparatus, furniture, or other article whatever, in the free schools of this State, or any one or more of them, or directly or indirectly contract for or receive any gift or reward for so introducing or recommending the same; *Shools officers and teachers not to act as agents.*

nor shall such person be otherwise interested in the sale,
proceeds or profits of any book or other thing used, or
to be used in said schools: *Provided*, That nothing
herein shall be construed to apply to any book written,
or thing invented by such person, or to merchants who,
in connection with their business, may desire to sell
school books or other things used in schools. *Provided,
further*, That the same are embrced in the prescribed
series.

CXXXVIII. It is not a violation of law for the teacher to order for the
pupils of his school, they furnishing the money, the lawful contract nchool
books they need, at the contract price, either by mail or express. The
teacher would violate the law, however, if he took any profit, or in any sense
became an agent or dealer in school books.

58. [This is inserted in place of section 58 of chapter
45 of the code, which is repealed by it.]
I. That on and after the first day of July, 1896, the
following text-books, and no others, except as hereinafter provided, shall be used in the primary and graded
schools throughout the State, and the prices of said
books shall be and remain the same as are named in this
section.

ORTHOGRAPHY.

Contract Price.

McGuffey's Revised Eclectic
Spelling Book............ 10c. (ten cents.)

READING.

Contract Price.

McGuffey's Revised First Ec-
lectic Reader............. 10c. (ten cents.)
McGuffey's Revised Second
Eclectic Reader........... 18c. (eighteen cents.)
McGuffey's Revised Third
Eclectic Reader........... 25c. (twenty-five cents.)
McGuffey's Revised Fourth
Eclectic Reader........... 30c. (thirty cents.)
McGuffey's Revised Fifth Ec-
lectic Reader............. 45c. (forty-five cents.)

PENMANSHIP.

Contract Price.

Ginn & Co.'s Grammar Course,
Nos. 1, 2, 3, 4, 5, 6 and 7, 32
pages to each number, Nos. 1
and 2 having two copies to each
page....................... 5c. each (five cts.)
Ginn & Co.'s Tracing Books, Nos.
1, 2 and 3................. 4c. each (four cts,

MATHEMATICS.

	Contract Price.	Contract Exchange Price.
Ray s New Primary Arithmetic.........	10c. (ten cents.)	
Brooks' New Mental Arithmetic..........	22c. (twenty-two cents.)	15c. (fifteen cents.)

	Contract Price.
Ray's New Practical Arithmetic	35c. (thirty-five cents.)
Ray's New Higher Arithmetic	60c. (sixty cents.)
Ray's New Elementary Algebra	60c. (sixty cents.)
Ray's New Higher Algebra...	75c. (seventy-five cents.)
Evans' School Geometry for beginners	40c. (forty cents.)

ENGLISH GRAMMAR.

	Contract Price.
Hyde's Language Lessons, Part I	25c. (twenty-five cts.)
Hyde's Language Lessons, Part II	43c. (forty:three cts.)

	Contract Price.	Contract Exchange Price.
Advanced Lessons in English (Hyde), for high schools........	36c. (thirty-six cents.)	25c. (twenty-five cents.)
Harvey's Revised English Grammar (Harvey), for high schools	47c. (forty-seven cents.)	

PHYSIOLOGY.

	Contract Price.
Cutter's Beginner's Anatomy, Physiology and Hygiene.....	20c. (twenty cents.)
Cutter's Intermediate Physiology and Hygiene............	35c. (thirty-five cents.)
Cutter's Comprehensive Physiology and Hygiene	60c. (sixty cents.)

HISTORY.

	Contract Price.	Contract Exchange Price.
General History— Myers' General History.	$1.10 (one dollar and ten cents.)	82c. (eighty-two cents.)

	Contract Price.	Exchange Price
United States—Leading Facts of American History (Montgomery)	65c. (sixty-five cents.)	50c. (fifty cents.)
The Beginner's American History (Montgomery)	43c. (forty-three .cents.)	35c. (thirty-five cents.)
State History—History and Government of West Virginia (Lewis)	80c. (eighty cents.)	

GEOGRAPHY.

	Contract Price.	Contract Exchange Price.
Mitchell's New Primary Geography	thirty-five cents per copy.	
Mitchell's New Intermediate Geography.	eighty cents per copy.	
Knote's Geography of West Virginia	thirty cents per copy.	
Maury's Physical Geography	75c. (seventy-five cents.)	25c. (twenty five cents.)
Butler's New Physical Geography	75c. (seventy-five cents.)	25c. (twenty five cents.)

SINGLE ENTRY BOOK-KEEPING.

	Contract Price.	Contract Exchange Price.
Meservey's Book-keeping	35c. (thirty-five cents.)	20c. (twenty cents.)
Meservey's Book-keeping Blanks (optional), per set.	35c. (thirty-five cents.)	

CIVIL GOVERNMENT.

	Contract Price.	Contract Exchange Price.
The American Citizen (Dole)	65c. (sixty-five cents.)	43c. forty-three cents.)

Provided, That "Dole's American Citizen" shall not

be contracted for under the provisions of this act, either as a work on civil government or as a reader, until the same has been changed so as to conform with the Senate resolution offered by Mr. Finley and adopted by the Senate on February 14, 1895.

MAPS.

Rand, McNally & Company's wall maps and school globes, 40 per cent. off retail price.

MISCELLANEOUS.

Contract Price.

Dictation Blanks, (O'Neill), Nos. 1, 2, and 3 each.............. 4c. (four cents).
Globe Practical Spelling Tablet 36 pages................... 3c. (three cents).

Optional Studies in Schools of all Grades.

OBJECT DRAWING.

Contract Price.

Jacob's and Brower's Elementary, Nos. 1, 2, 3, 4, per copy.... 8c. (eight cents).
Advanced, Nos. 5, 6, 7, per copy. 11c. (eleven cents).
Teachers' Manual............. 30c. (thirty cents).

MUSIC.

Contract Price.

Cecilian Series of Study and Song, No. 1................ 25c. (twenty-five cents.)
Cecilian Series of Study and Song, No. 2................ 35c. (thirty-five cents.)
Cecilian Series of Study and Song, No. 3................ 50c. (fifty cents.)
Cecilian Series of Study and Song, No. 4................ 50c. (fifty cents.)

SUPPLEMENTARY READING.

Contract Price.

Nature Readers, Book I. (Wright) .... 18c (eighteen cents.)
Nature Readers, Book II. (Wright) .... 25c (twenty-five cents.)
Nature Readers, Book III. (Wright) .... 38c (thirty-eight cents.)
Nature Readers, Book IV. (Wright) .... 45c (forty-five cents.)

Works of Reference.

DICTIONARIES.

(1) Webster's Common School....$0.50 (fifty cents.)
(2) Webster's Academic......... 1.00 (one dollar.)
(1) Worcester's New School...... .55 (fifty-five cents.)
(2) Worcester's Academic........ 1.00 (one dollar.)
Peter's Tellurian with Instruction
    Book....................... 5.00 (five dollars.)

Provided, That no pupil or school shall be required by any board of education, teacher or trustee to use the supplementary reading books, dictation blanks, Cecilian Series of Study and Song, Peter's Tellurian with Instruction Book, Globe Practical Spelling Tablet, Rand, McNally & Co.'s wall maps, or object drawing, unless the parent or guardian of said pupil elect to do so, and no depositary shall be required to keep the same on hand for sale.

II. The State Superintendent of schools shall, on or before the first day of September, one thousand eight hundred and ninety-five, contract with the several publishers for the text books named in the preceding section, or that may be adopted under the provisions of this act, for supplying such books for use in the free schools of the State.

State Superintendent to contract for books.

III. The text-books selected and prescribed under the provisions of this act shall be sold by said publishers to any board of education, depositary, teacher, pupil, parent or guardian or other person of this State at a price not exceeding the net contract price named in connection with and opposite each of said books in section one of this act. Such contract shall be made for a period of five years, beginning with the first day of July, eighteen hundred and ninety-six, and shall also provide that said publishers will supply such books in sufficient quantities and in quality of paper, typography and binding equal to the sample copies exhibited to the committees on education of the session of the Legislature of this State of one thousand eight hundred and ninety-five, and shall provide that said publishers shall deposit with said State Superintendent similar copies of said books, to be properly marked and safely kept by him.

Contract for five years.

Other conditions of contract.

No revision of such books shall be introduced into the free schools of this State during the life of the contract, except that the publishers of said geographies may make such changes therein, but not so as to alter the arrangement thereof, as may be necessary to cause such

Changes in books.

books to conform to the facts of later explorations, the changes in the form of government and political divisions, and the discoveries of science.

Said contract shall also provide that said publishers shall print for the information of county superintendents, boards of education and for general circulation, a full schedule of the contract prices and exchange prices agreed upon, and to furnish to each county superintendent so many copies of such schedule as may not be less than the aggregate number of school houses and places in the county where such books are sold. Such contracts with the publishers of books not now used in the schools of this State, shall provide for furnishing such books at the exchange prices named opposite said books in section one (1) of this act; and that said publishers shall make no charge to the boards of education or depositaries or other persons for the boxing or cartage of such books, but shall deliver the same free on board cars at the place of publication; and that the said publishers shall at the end of the life of any contract that may be made under the provision of this act, take back all copies of their books that may be in the hands of said depositaries and in good condition, and refund the amount paid therefor; also that if any of said publishers shall hereafter furnish any of said books to any state, county, district or township, city or town, at less than the foregoing prices, then such decreased prices shall also be established as a part of any contract made under the provisions of this act. *Schedule of prices.*

IV. The several publishers of the said described school books shall each, on or before the first day of September, one thousand eight hundred and ninety-five, execute and file with the State Superintendent of Schools, a bond to be approved by the Governor, in the penalty of ten thousand dollars, payable to the State of West Virginia, conditioned according to law for the faithful performance of the contract and agreement made in pursuance with this act. And upon a breach of any of the conditions of such bond, the State Superintendent shall, in the name of the State, institute suit thereon to recover for the same. All moneys so recovered, after the payment of the costs of such proceedings, shall be paid into the general school fund and be distributed with it as provided by law. *Publishers' bond.*

V. If any publishers of any of said text books, or series of such books, as are published in a series, shall fail or refuse on or before the first day of September, one thousand eight hundred and ninety-five, to agree and contract, and execute and file bond as hereinbefore required, it shall be the duty of the Governor to appoint *Failure or refusal to contract.*

three persons, citizens of this State, not more than two of whom shall be of the same political party, to be known as the State School Book Board, to solicit proposals from any publisher for the furnishing of such books not contracted for as may be required to complete the list of text-books for use in the free schools of the State; and from the books so offered, they shall select such as in their judgment are best adapted to be used in said schools, and to contract before the first day of July, one thousand eight hundred and ninety-six, for the furnishing of the same in conformity with the provisions of this act.

Provided, That said School Book Board shall not contract for any text-book at a price exceeding the price named in section one of this act for books on the same subject, but may, in their discretion, require publishers to exchange books so contracted for on a free or even exchange for those now in use.

The said State School Book Board shall each receive four dollars per day each day, not to exceed twenty-five days, they are necessarily employed in carrying out the provisions of this act, and actual necessary traveling ing expenses, to be paid by the Auditor out of the general fund, on the certificate and order of said State School Book Board. Any vacancy in said board shall be filled by the Governor.

VI. At the first meeting after the 30th day of June, 1896, the board of education of every district in this state, shall appoint one or more depositaries in each district, and when practicable one or more depositaries at or near each postoflice, whereat shall be kept at all times a sufficient supply of text-books to supply the free schools of the neighborhood. Each depositary shall execute a bond in the penalty of double the value of the books which he will probably have on hand at any time, but in no event of a less penalty than two hundred dollars; which bond shall be approved by the board of education and filed with the secretary thereof.

VII. Each depositary shall, on or before the first day of September following, unless the board of education shall name an earlier date, make out a list of the textbooks, in sufficient quantity in his judgment, to supply the schools of his neighborhood for a period of six months, and from time to time thereafter each depositary shall make out additional lists of such books so that he may at all times have a sufficient supply on hand; such lists, when approved by the board of education, or the president thereof, shall be signed by him and the secretary thereof, and by the secretary forwarded to the address of the publishers of the books therein named.

School Book Board.

Remuneration of Book Board.

Depositaries.

Depositaries to make lists of books.

VIII. It shall be the duty of said publishers promptly to forward the books therein named to such depository, and to make out two invoices or bills therefor, one of which shall be forwarded to the depositary and the other to the secretary of the board of education. The board of education shall supply the secretary with a proper book in which to keep the accounts of all the depositaries in the district. On the receipt of each invoice the secretary shall charge the amount thereof against the depositary receiving the books therein named in said account book, and file or preserve the invoice or bill. If there be any error in such invoice or bill, the depositary receiving the same, shall promptly notify the publisher making the same, and if such publisher fail to correct such error within ten days thereafter, such depositary shall notify the secretary of the board of education thereof, and the board of education shall investigate the same and take such action therein as may be proper and just. *Invoices of books.*

Each depository shall pay to the sheriff of the county, at the end of each sixty days, or oftener if required, and whenever required by the board of education, the amount of money received by him from the sale of such text-books, since his last previous payment, less his commission, not exceeding twelve per cent. on the account of such sales. *Depositaries' commission.*

The sheriff shall give duplicate receipts therefor to such depository, wherein shall be stated the total amount of such sales and the amount paid by such depositary to the sheriff, one of which receipts shall be filed by such depositary with the secretary of the board of education; and upon receiving the same, said secretary shall credit the account of said depositary with the amount appearing thereby to have been so paid by him, and the amount of said commission, by separate items; and said secretary shall charge against the account of the sheriff, which he is hereby required to keep, the amount paid by such depositary to such sheriff, to be accounted for by the sheriff in his annual settlement with the board of education. *Sheriff's receipts, &c.*

The amounts received from the sales of such books, shall be credited to the building fund of the district. Each depository shall be allowed a commission not to exceed twelve per cent. on the amount of all sales made by him, out of which commission he shall be required to pay all charges for transportation. *Money from sale of books.*

IX. The board of education of each district shall be liable in its corporate capacity for the whole amount of all such text-books furnished to the depositaries in the manner hereinbefore prescribed, and shall within sixty *Board of Education liable.*

days from the date of any invoice or bill of text-books supplied by the publishers thereof to any depositary in the district, in the manner prescribed in the preceding section, cause an order to be issued in favor of such publishers, payable out of the building fund of the district, and cause such order to be forwarded by mail to such publishers. On presentation of such order to him the sheriff shall pay the amount thereof to the party entitled to receive the same, if there be in his hands sufficient funds due the building fund of said district; but if the sheriff have not sufficient of such funds to pay the same, he shall endorse on the back thereof the words "Presented for payment," with the date of such presentation, and said order shall draw interest from that date. If the sheriff shall fail or refuse to pay such order when he has funds in his hands, or should by law have the same, with which to do so, he shall be liable as provided in section forty-six of chapter forty-five of the code.

Levy for books.

X. The board of education shall pay the cost of such text-books out of the building fund of the district, and shall lay an annual levy for the same on the taxable property of the district, in the manner and at the time that other levies are laid for said fund.

State Superintendent to prepare blank forms.

XI. It shall be the duty of the State Superintendent of Schools to prepare and have printed a form of bond to be executed by the depositaries, blank order lists for books, which shall contain the names and titles and prices of all books contracted for under the provisions of this act, and the names and addresses of the publishers thereof, and also such other blanks, and also instructions as in his judgment may be deemed necessary to cause the provisions of this act to be carried out in a proper manner. He shall furnish to each County Superintendent a sufficient supply thereof for his county.

Names and addresses of presidents and secretaries.

XII. It shall be the duty of the County Superintendent of every county, on or before the first day of July, eighteen hundred and ninety-six, to furnish to every publisher of text-books contracted with under the provisions of this act, the names and post-office addresses of all the presidents and secretaries of boards of education in his county; and he shall notify such publishers of any changes in such names and addresses as soon as they shall come to his knowledge.

Board may remove Depositary.

XIII. The board of education may remove any depositary in its district at any time, and appoint another in his stead; may require him to execute a new bond, or additional bond, whenever in their opinion they shall deem it necessary, and may cause to be made at any time an invoice of said text-books in the possession of any such depositary. It shall be the duty of every depositary, whenever the board of education shall so order, to turn over to his successor, or such other person as the said board may name, all such text-books in his possession.

XIV. Depositaries shall receive from any resident of this State copies of the books that are or may be superseded by the provisions of this act, at the contract exchange prices, named in section one (1) of this act or as provided for under the provisions of section five (5) of this act, to be applied on payment of the prescribed books. Each depositary shall turn over all such old books to the board of education at such times as said board may direct, and shall be credited on his account with the value thereof. Said old books shall be held by the board of education subject to the orders of the publishers, for a period of not longer than three months. *Books in exchange.*

XV. If any teacher in a primary or graded school of the free school system of the State use or cause to be used in such primary or graded school, any text-books not herein authorized, then in any such case or instance, any publisher of a text-book which should have been used in the place of such unauthorized text-books may apply to the State Superintendent of Free Schools for an order signed by him, to be directed to such teacher requiring the use of such unauthorized class-book to be discontinued; which order it shall be the duty of the State Superintendent of Free Schools to give to such publisher upon his affidavit or that of his agent setting forth the name of the teacher, the location and character of the school, the title or the name of the unauthorized text-book, and stating that such teacher is using such unauthorized text-book in such school. *Teacher liable.*

XVI. If the State Superintendent of Free Schools shall refuse to give to any publisher entitled thereto, such an order within fifteen days after application made therefor, such publisher shall, if the facts stated in the affidavit are true, be entitled to a mandamus from the Supreme Court of Appeals to compel the State Superintendent of Free Schools to give such order. In any proceedings in mandamus brought hereunder, it shall be the duty of the Attorney-General to act as counsel for the State Superintendent of Free Schools, but such proceedings shall be at the cost of such publisher, and in no case shall costs be recovered against the State Superintendent or against any teacher. *State Superintendent liable.*

XVII. If any teacher shall disobey any order issued by the State Superintendent of Free Schools under the provisions of section four of this act, such teacher shall *Forfeit.*

forfeit ten dollars, and it shall be the duty of the board of education of the district where the teacher is employed to retain that amount out of the salary of such teacher, which amount so forfeited shall be paid into the teachers' fund of such district.

Hyde's language books, grammars.

XVIII. Hyde's Lesson Books I. and II., and Hyde's Advanced Lessons in English, are hereby declared to be English grammars within the meaning of all the provisions of chapter forty-five of the Code of West Virginia.

Misdemeanor.

XIX. Any publisher, school officer, teacher or other person violating any of the provisions of this act, shall be deemed guilty of a misdemeanor and on conviction thereof, shall be fined for each offense not less than ten dollars or more than fifty dollars.

Acts repealed.

XX. Sections 58 and 58a of chapter 45 of the code of West Virginia, and all other acts or parts of acts inconsistent with the provisions of this act are hereby repealed.

58a. [Passed February 19, 1897.]

School Book Board.

I. There is hereby established in every county of this State a school book board, to be composed of the county superintendent of the county, who shall be a member and the secretary of the board and eight other reputable citizens and taxpayers of the county. At least four of the eight shall be freeholders and not school teachers, and at least three shall be persons actively engaged as teachers in the schools of the county, and shall hold a teacher's number one certificate or its equivalent. Not more than five of said eight shall belong to the same political party. The said eight persons shall be appointed by the county court. The term of office of each of said members shall be four years and until their successors are appointed, beginning on the first day of July next after their appointment. Said appointment shall be made on or before the fifteenth day of June, one thousand eight hundred and ninety-seven, and in every fourth year thereafter on or before the fifteenth day of July, and the term of office of those appointed after the first appointments (except appointments to fill vacancies) shall begin on the first day of August next after their appointment, and continue four years and until their successors are appointed. They shall receive as compensation for their services the sum of two dollars per day for each day they shall be in session as a board, and shall not receive pay for more than two days in any one year, which compensation shall be paid out of the county treasury. Vacancies in said board shall be filled for the unexpired term in the same manner as the original appointment was made. Five members shall constitute a quorum,

How appointed; term of office.

When appointed.

Compensation.

Vacancies.

Quorum.

but a smaller number may adjourn from day to day until a quorum appears. Every person so appointed shall, before entering upon his duties, take an oath that he will support the Constitution of the United States and the Constitution of West Virginia, and that he will faithfully discharge the duties of his office. A certificate of every such oath shall be filed with and preserved by the clerk of the county court.

II. The secretary shall keep a record, in a book pro- Secretary. vided for the purpose, of the transactions of every meetof the board, and shall record the names of the members voting for and against every proposition to adopt any text-book; which record shall be open to the inspection of any citizen of the county.

III. Immediately after the appointment of said board, in the year one thousand eight hundred and ninety-seven, it shall be the duty of the county superintendent to communicate with the publishers of text books, inviting the submission by such publishers of samples and prices of their books. When such samples and prices have been obtained, it shall be the duty of said board to meet at the county seat on or before the first Monday of August, First meetin . one thousand eight hundred and ninety-seven, on the call of the county superintendent, and organize by choosing one of their number president. Said board shall then proceed to select and adopt one text book, or a series of text-books, on each subject required to be taught in the free schools of the State, and not provided for by contract under chapter thirty-seven of the Acts of one thousand eight hundred and ninety-five, for a term of five years, due reference being had to the character of the books and the terms offered. It shall require the affirmative votes of five members of the board to adopt such book, or series of books, at said first meeting.

IV. In making selection of text-books, at any time, it Retail price, shall be the duty of said board to procure the best poss- &c. ible terms for exchange and introduction and for the regular supply of the books for a term of five years, and they are hereby empowered to fix the retail price at which such adopted books shall be sold after the exchange and introduction have been effected, but such permanent retail price shall not exceed twenty-five per cent. advance on the net contract price.

V. Said board shall, upon making an adoption of any Secretary to text-books, decide upon the date when such adoption report. shall go into effect. The secretary shall send to the State Superintendent of Free Schools, and to all the boards of education in the county, notice of the names of the books adopted, the prices fixed therefor, and the date fixed for their introduction and use in the schools of the county.

Meeting before expiration of contract. VI. At least six months before the expiration of the contract made under provisions of chapter thirty-seven of the Acts of one thousand eight hundred and ninety-five, it shall be the duty of the State Superintendent to notify the county superintendent of every county of the date of the expiration of such contracts and the name of the text-books thereby affected; and it shall be the duty of said board to meet upon the call of the county superintendent, at least three months before the expiration of any such contract, and adopt one text-book, or a series of text-books, on each subject contracted for under said chapter thirty-seven of the Acts of one thousand eight hundred and ninety-five, for a term of five years. On the call of the county superintendent, **County Superintendent to call meeting.** the board shall meet in regular session at least three months before the expiration of any contract made under the provisions of this act, and select the necessary books to be used for the succeeding term of five years. If any publisher shall fail or refuse to furnish any book contracted for under the provisions of this act, it shall be the duty of the said board, on the call of the county superintendent, to meet and select books to be used instead of those which said publishers have failed or refused to furnish. But no books shall thereafter be adopted of a publisher who shall have failed or re- **Refusal of publishers to carry out contract.** fused to fulfil his contract with any board in the State, and the name of any such publisher shall be furnished by the secretary of said board to the State Superintendent of Free Schools, and the State Superintendent shall communicate the same to every county superintendent.

Present contract to remain in force. VII. No text-book or series of text-books, on any one subject now contracted for under said chapter thirty-seven of the Acts of one thousand eight hundred and ninety-five, or that shall be contracted for under the provisions of this act, shall be changed for another or different book or series of books except by the affirmative votes of five members of the board: *Provided*, That no change in the text-books contracted for under the provisions of said chapter thirty-seven of the acts of one thousand eight hundred and ninety-five shall be made until the expiration of such contracts, unless for failure of the contractor. And not more than one book **Not more than one book changed, except.** or one series of books on one subject, shall be changed in any one year, except by the affirmative votes of six members, and except as provided in section three: *Provided*, That in case of failure of a publisher to comply with his contract, the board may, by the affirmative vote .

of five members, adopt other books in place of those contracted for.

VIII. After the adoption of any text-books the board shall contract with the publishers proposing the same, to supply said books in sufficient quantities, for a term of five years, beginning on a date to be stated in the contract, to every board of education, depositary, agent of said school book board or of said board of education, or to any dealer or other person of the county, at the prices named in this contract, and free on board the cars at the place of publication or other place (which place shall be named in such contract); and that said books shall be equal in binding, typography, and in all other respects to the samples furnished; and that no changes shall be made in said book during the life of the contract. In such contract shall be stated the accurate title of every book therein contracted for, the name of the author and of the publisher thereof, and the agreed price or prices thereof. Forms of such contract shall be prepared by the State Superintendent of Free Schools, and furnished to each county superintendent. Every dealer or publisher entering into such a contract. shall furnish to the county superintendent a sample copy of each book contracted for, and the county superintendent shall attach to each of said books a label bearing thereon: "Sample copy contracted for with ....
on the ...... day of ...., 189..
................, County Superintendent." *(margin note: Who may sell books.)* *(margin note: Form of contract.)*

IX. Every publisher entering into contract with any board under the provisions of this act, shall, within thirty days thereafter, give a bond, in the penalty of ten thousand dollars, to be approved by the Governor and deposited ;with the State Superintendent of Free Schools, conditioned for the faithful performance of every such contract made by such publisher theretofore or thereafter with any such board. *(margin note: Bond of publisher.)*

X. No member of said board shall serve, directly or indirectly, as the agent for any publisher in school books competing for adoption under the provisions of this act, or be personally interested in any school book, and no teacher nor school officer shall act as agent for any school book. *(margin note: No school officer act as agent.)*

XI. At the first meeting after the thirtieth day of June, one thousand eight hundred and ninety-seven, the board of education of any district in this State may (at their option) appoint one or more depositaries in each district, and when practicable one or more depositaries at or near each postoffice, who shall keep at all times a sufficient supply of text-books to supply the free schools of the neighborhood. Each depositary shall execute a *(margin note: Depositaries.)*

Bond of Depositary.

bond in the penalty of double the value of the books which he will probably have on hand at any time, but in no event of a less penalty than one hundred dollars; which bond shall be approved by the board of education and filed with the secretary thereof. The board of education may discharge any depositary at any time, and require him to deliver the books in his possession to such person as the board may name, and require the depositary to settle his accounts and pay over to the sheriff any balance in his hands on or before a date named by the board.

Depositary to keep books.

XII. Each depositary shall, on or before the first day of September in each year, unless the board of education shall name an earlier date, make out a list of the text-books, in sufficient quantity in his judgment to supply the schools in his neighborhood for a period of six months, and from time to time thereafter each depositary shall make out additional lists of such books, so that he may at all times have a sufficient supply on hand; such lists, when approved by the board of education, or the president thereof, shall be signed by him and the secretary thereof, and by the secretary forwarded to the address of the publishers of the books therein named.

Invoices of books.

XIII. It shall be the duty of said publishers promptly to forward the books therein named to such depositary, and to make out two invoices or bills therefor, one of which shall be forwarded to the depositary and the other to the secretary of the board of education. The board of education shall supply the secretary with a proper book in which to keep the accounts of all the depositaries in the district. On the receipt of each invoice the secretary shall charge the amount thereof against the depositary receiving the books therein named, in said account book, and file or preserve the invoice or bill. If there be any error in such invoice or bills, the depositary receiving the same shall promptly notify the publisher making the same; and if such publisher fail to correct such error within twenty days thereafter, such depositary shall notify the secretary of the board of education thereof, and the board of education shall investigate the same and take such action therein as may be proper and just. Each depositary shall pay to the

Payment to the sheriff.

sheriff of the county, at the end of each thirty days, or oftener if required, and whenever required by the board of education, the amount received by him from the sale of such text-books since his last previous payment, less

Depositary's commission.

his commission (to be fixed by the board of education and not to exceed fifteen per cent. on the amount of such sales), and the amount paid by him for transportation charges on such books; *provided*, that each statement of charges to the sheriff shall be accompanied by all the transportation bills paid by said depositary. The sheriff shall duplicate receipts therefor to such depositary, wherein shall be stated the total amount of such sales and the amount paid by such depositary to the sheriff, one of which receipts shall be filed by such depositary with the secretary of the board of eduction, and upon receiving the same said secretary shall credit the account of said depositary with the amount appearing thereby to have been so paid by him to the sheriff and the amount paid for transportation charges, and the amount of said commission by separate items, and said secretary shall charge against the account of the sheriff, which he is hereby required to keep, the amount paid by such depositary to such sheriff, to be accounted for by the sheriff in his annual settlement with the board of education. The amounts received from the sales of such books shall be credited to the building fund of the district.

XIV. The board of education of each district shall be liable in its corporate capacity for the whole amount of all such text-books furnished to the depositaries in the manner hereinbefore prescribed, and shall within sixty days from the date of any invoice or bill of text-books supplied by the publishers thereof to any depositary in the district in the manner prescribed in the preceding section, cause an order to be issued in favor of such publisher, payable out of the building fund of the district, and cause such order to be forwarded by mail to such publishers. On presentation of such order to him the sheriff shall pay the amount thereof to the party entitled to receive the same, if there be in his hands sufficient funds due the building fund of said district; but if the sheriff have not sufficient of such funds to pay the same, he shall endorse on the back thereof the words "Presented for payment," with the date of such presentation and said order shall draw interest from that date. *[margin: Board of Education liable.]*

If the Sheriff shall fail or refuse to pay such order when he has funds in his hands, or should by law have the same, with which to do so, he shall be liable as provided in section forty-six of chapter forty-five of the Code.

XV. The board of education shall pay the cost of such books and the amount of charges for transportation out of the building fund of the district, and shall lay an annual levy for the same upon the taxable property of the district in the manner and at the time that other levies are laid for said fund, and if at any time any *[margin: Books paid for out of Building Fund.]*

scholar or scholars should remove from the county into another county in which a different book, or series of books, or different books have been adopted, the board of education of any district are authorized to purchase from such scholar or scholars with money from the building fund and at a fair valuation, such book or books or series of books as may not be adopted in the county to which they may remove: *Provided,* That the provisions of this section shall not apply to districts in which no depository shall be appointed.

Board may remove depositary. XVI. The board of education may remove any depositary in his district at any time, and appoint another in his stead; may require him to execute a new bond, or additional bond, whenever in their opinion they shall deem it necessary, and may cause to be made at any time an invoice of the text-books in the possession of any such depository. It shall be the duty of every depositary whenever the board of education shall order, to turn over to his successor or such other person as the said board may name, all text-books in his possession.

Books in exchange. XVII. Every depositary shall receive from any resident of his district copies of the books that may at any time be superseded by adoption of other books in their stead, at the contract exchange allowance of such superseded books, to be applied on payment of adopted books. Each depositary shall turn over such superseded books to the board of education at such times as the board may direct, and shall receive credit on his account for the value thereof. Such superseded books shall be held by the board of education subject to the orders of the publishers thereof, for a period of not longer than three months.

Teacher liable. XVIII. If any teacher in a primary or graded school of the free school system of this State use, or cause to be used in such primary or graded school, any text-books not authorized in place of an authorized book, then the county superintendent shall apply to the board of education for an order signed by said board, directed to such teacher, requiring the use of such unauthorized text-book to be discontinued; and if any teacher shall disobey any such order issued by said board of education, such teacher shall forfeit the sum of ten dollars for each such offense, and it shall be the duty of the board of. education of the district where said teacher is employed to retain that amount out of the salary of said teacher, which amount so forfeited shall be paid into the teachers' fund of such district.

Misdemeanor. XIX. Any publisher, school officer, depositary, dealer, teacher or other person, violating the provisions of this act, shall be guilty of a misdemeanor, and, on

conviction thereof, shall be fined for each offense not
less than five nor more than fifty dollars.

XX. Nothing contained in this act shall be construed Acts repealed.
as changing or modifying the contracts heretofore made
with publishers of text-books under authority of chapter thirty-seven of the Acts of one thousand eight hundred and ninety-five; and all acts, or parts of acts, coming within the purview of this act and inconsistent therewith, are hereby repealed.

59. If any officer or teacher, fail to perform any duty Fines for
required of him by this chapter, or violate any provis- violations.
ion thereof, and there is no other fine or punishment
imposed therefor, by law, he shall be fined not less than
three, nor more than ten dollars, for every such offense,
to be recovered before a justice of the peace of the
county; and such fine shall not impair or affect his liability for damages to any person injured, nor the liability of himself and sureties on his official bond. If the
board of education of any district or independent school
district, fail to perform any duty required by this act,
each member of such board shall be liable to the full
penalty imposed by this section, unless he show that he
was not guilty of any neglect or default in the premises.

60. For the support of free schools, there shall be a State school
state tax levied, annually, of ten cents on the one hun- tax.
dred dollars' valuation on all the real and personal property of the State, which, together with the interest of
the invested school fund, the net proceeds of all forfeitures, confiscations and fines which accrued to the State
during the previous year, the proceeds of the annual
capitation tax, dividends on bank stock held by the
board of the school fund, and the interest accruing on
stock invested in United States bonds, shall be set apart
as a separate fund to be called "the general school "General
fund," and shall be annually applied to the support of School Fund."
free schools throughout the State, and to no other purpose whatever. It shall be distributed to the several
counties in the State in proportion to the number of
youth therein, according to the latest enumeration made
for school purposes; but the auditor shall first deduct
therefrom the aggregate salary of the State Superintendent of Free Schools, and the necessary traveling
and contingent expenses of his office, together with such
other sums as may be required to be paid by him out of
the general school fund. Fifty per cent. of this distributable sum shall be paid on the fifteenth day of Sep- When
tember, and the remainder on the fifteenth day of De- distributed.
cember, of each year, and in the manner provided in the
sixty-first section of this chapter.

61. It shall be the duty of the auditor, on or before

the tenth day of June, in each year, to ascertain the amount which is distributable among the several counties as aforesaid, and notify the State Superintendent of Free Schools thereof, who shall thereupon ascertain the proper share of each county and notify the auditor and each county superintendent, also, the amount deducted by the auditor from the share of his county on account of salary paid the county superintendent, as required by section fifty-four, which amount the county superintendent shall also deduct from the share of his county before making his distribution of the same among the several districts thereof.

Upon receiving such notice, the county superintendent shall ascertain the proper share of each district, and independent school district, of his county, according to the number of youths therein, and give notice to the board of education of each district, and independent school district, in the county, of the amount of the general school fund due each, respectively, and that the same cannot be drawn by them until they have made the levy required by the fortieth section of this chapter.

62. Upon being officially notified by the secretary of the board of education, in the manner provided for in the forty-fourth section of this chapter, that the board of education has authorized the levy for school purposes, the county superintendent shall issue his requisition on the auditor, payable to the order of the sheriff of his county for the amounts due such districts as may have made the levy aforesaid, which shall be paid in two equal installments, payable on the fifteenth days of September and December, respectively; whereupon the auditor shall issue his warrant upon the treasurer in favor of the sheriff for the amount of such requisition, indicating in writing upon said warrant the depositary upon which the same shall be drawn; and the treasurer shall thereupon be authorized and required to draw his check upon the said depositary for the said amount.

The requisition of the county superintendent shall be in form or in substance as follows:

OFFICE OF THE COUNTY SUPERINTENDENT OF FREE SCHOOLS,

County of ——, the ——— day of ——, 18- .

Auditor of West Virginia:

Pay to the order of ————————, sheriff of ——— ———— county, ———— dollars, the amount of State school fund apportioned to the district (or independent school district) of ————, in said county for the year 18—.

And I hereby certify that said district (or independent school district), has made the levy required by law, for school purposes, and that said sheriff has given the bond required by law.

A—— ——B ——.——, County Superintendent of Schools."

CXXXIX. Sections 42 and 61 prohibit any district or independent school district from receiving its proportion of the State school fund, until it has laid the local levy required by section 40. County superintendents should inform the Auditor if a district votes down the levy that he may act in compliance with section 42.

63. There shall be elected a State Superintendent of Free Schools for the State, whose term of office shall be the same as that of the Governor. He shall be a person of good moral character, of temperate habits, of literary acquirements, and skill and experience in the art of teaching. He shall receive annually the sum of one thousand five hundred dollars in payment for his services, to be paid monthly out of the school fund upon the warrant of the Auditor. If in the performance of any duty imposed upon him by the Legislature, he shall incur any expenses, he shall be reimbursed therefor. *Provided*, The amount does not exceed five hundred dollars in any one year.

State Superintendent.

64. The State Superintendent shall reside and keep his office at the seat of government. He shall provide a seal for his office, and copies of his acts and decisions, and of papers kept in his office, authenticated by his signature and official seal shall be evidence equally with the original. He shall sign all requisitions on the Auditor for the payment of money out of the State treasury for school purposes, except as hereinafter provided.

ate Superintendent.

65. The State Superintendent shall be charged with the supervision of all county superintendents and free schools of the State, and see that the school system is carried into effect. He shall prepare and transmit to the county superintendents instructions how to conduct the elections prescribed in this chapter, to keep and transmit the official records and ballots thereof, and the manner of ascertaining and announcing the results, so as to conform the same to the provisions of this chapter, and also to such provisions of the general election laws of the State as may not be inconsistent therewith; he shall prescribe and cause to be prepared all forms and blanks necessary in the details of the system, so as to secure its uniform operation throughout the State, and shall cause the same to be forwarded to the several county superintendents, to be by them distributed to the persons entitled to the same. He shall cause as many copies of this chapter and other school laws in force with such forms, regulations and instructions as he may judge

Duties of State Superintendent.

expedient, thereto annexed, to be from time to time published, as he may deem expedient, and shall cause the same to be forwarded to the county superintendents, to be by them distributed to the persons entitled to receive them.

Duties of State Superintendent.

66. It shall be the duty of the State Superintendent to aim at perfecting the system of free schools as established in the State; and for this purpose it shall be his duty to correspond with educators and school officers abroad, to acquaint himself with the various systems of free schools established in other states and countries, collate the results as exhibited in the reports of their several superintendents, and to use all efforts necessary to enable him to render available the combined results of the experience of other communities with his own experience and observation.

He shall acquaint himself intimately with the peculiar educational wants of each section of the State, and shall take all proper means to supply them, so that the schools shall be as nearly as possible equal and uniform in grade throughout the State. He shall acquaint himself with the different systems and methods of instruction which may be introduced among educators, and shall explain and recommend such as experience and sound principles of education may have demonstrated to be valuable; and it shall be his duty to endeavor to render available to the people of this State all such improvements in the system of free schools and the methods of instruction, as may have been tested and proven by the experience of other communities.

Report of State Superintendent.

67. He shall, on or before the first day of January, of each year, make a report to the Governor, to be by him transmitted to the next regular session of the Legislature, in regard to the condition of free schools within the State, embracing all statistics compiled from the reports of the county superintendents, and such other authentic information as he can procure, which will be necessary to give a proper exhibit of the working of the system together with such plans as he may have matured for the management and improvement of the school fund, and for the better and more perfect organization and efficiency of free schools; and, likewise, all such matters in relation to his office and to free schools, as he may deem expedient to communicate.

Auditor to report condition of school fund.

68. The Auditor shall annually, before the first day of September, deliver to the Governor and the State Superintendent of Free Schools, each, a report made up to the first day of July next preceding, of the condition of "the school fund," with an abstract of the accounts thereof in his office, which report the Governor

shall lay before the legislature at its next regular session.

CXL. Chapter 29, section 67, Code, requires the Auditor to certify to each county superintendent the amount of railroad levies, due to each district and independent district. See said section.

69. The Governor, State Superintendent of Free Schools, Auditor and Treasurer, shall be a corporation, under the name of "the board of the school fund," and shall have the management, control and investment of said fund, under the fourth section of the twelfth article of the constitution. The Governor shall be president of the board, and in his absence the board may choose one of their number to preside temporarily in his place. The Auditor shall be the secretary of the board. A faithful record shall be kept of all the proceedings, and a copy thereof, certified by the secretary of the board, shall be evidence in all cases in which the original would be. A majority of the board shall constitute a quorum for the transaction of business. *Board of school fund.*

70. A meeting of the board may be held at any time, upon the call of any member thereof, provided notice be given to all members who may be at the seat of government. The auditor's office shall be the place of meeting, and the proceedings shall be signed by the president and secretary of the meeting for that day, and shall be open to inspection at all times. *Meetings.*

71. All the money which ought to be paid into the treasury to the credit of "the school fund" shall be recoverable with interest by action or motion in the name of said board, before any court having jurisdiction, and the attorney-general shall institute and prosecute such action or motion when so directed by the board. *Money recoverable.*

72. The board may appoint agents for the collection of debts or claims, and authorize them to secure payment thereof, and to protect the interests of the school fund, on such terms as it may approve. They shall take bond from said agent, if any money is to come into his hands; and any agent selling lands, when directed to do so by the board, shall execute a deed, (with the resolution giving such directions thereto annexed), conveying to the purchaser by special warranty. Said agent may be allowed by the board a compensation not exceeding, in any case, five per cent. on the money paid into the treasury. *Board may appoint agents.*

73. All such sums as have accrued or shall hereafter accrue to this State, from the several sources enumerated in the fourth section of the twelfth article of the Constitution, shall be set apart as a separate fund to be called "the school fund," and it shall be the duty of the auditor to ascertain from time to time what sums have *Permanent school fund; how invested.*

so accrued or may hereafter accrue, and to pass the same to the credit of the said school fund; and it shall be the duty of the board of the school fund, from time to time, to invest the same in the interest bearing securities of the United States, or of this State, or otherwise, provided for in said fourth section of the twelfth article of the Constitution. And it shall be the duty of the said board to sell any investments on account of the school fund now made in other securities, than those required in said fourth section of the twelfth article of the Constitution, and invest the proceeds thereof in the interest bearing securities of the United States, or of this State, or otherwise, as provided in the Constitution aforesaid.

Certain stocks transferred to school fund.

(73a I. All stock owned by the state of West Virginia, standing in the name of the Commonwealth of Virginia, the State Internal Improvement Fund, or the Board of the Literary Fund, or in any other name, in the National Bank of West Virginia, at Wheeling, the Parkersburg National Bank, the First National Bank of Wellsburg, the First National Bank of Fairmont, the National Exchange Bank of Weston, and all the interest owned by the State, standing in the name of the Commonwealth of Virginia, or in the name of either of said funds, or in the name of the State of West Virginia, or in any other name, in the North Western Bank of Virginia and its branches, and in the branches of the Exchange Bank of Virginia at Weston; and all dividends and accrued interest on all such stock, is hereby transferred to and shall henceforth be held and treated as a part of the school fund of the State, subject to the control of the board of the school fund; and the annual interest or profits thereof (but no part of the principal), shall be passed to and become a part of the fund for annual distribution among the several counties of the State.)

Auditor shall be accountant.

74. The auditor shall be the accountant of the board, exercising any of their powers, except that he shall not, without special authority, entered upon the records of their proceedings, dispose of any property or invest any money of the school fund. He shall place the securities in which said school fund is invested in such depository for safe keeping, as the board shall direct. All money belonging to "the school fund" shall be received into and paid out of the treasury upon the warrant of the auditor. But no warrant for paying out such money shall be issued without the authority of the board.

75. Nothing in this chapter shall alter or affect the laws now in force respecting the free schools in the city

of Wheeling, and the parts of districts connected there- City of Wheeling. with; nor shall anything in this chapter be construed as abolishing any independent school district heretofore created, or as affecting any right or privilege conferred upon them, respectively, in the acts of the legislature by which they have been created; except so far as such right or privilege may be inconsistent with the provisions of this chapter in which independent school districts are especially included. In the independent school district of Wheeling none but practical educators who shall have had at least three years of practice as teachers in graded schools, shall be eligible to the office of superintendent.

CXLI. Independent school districts are those created by special act of the Legislature and are governed by the laws laid down in the acts creating them. On points where these acts are silent the general law applies. The principal independent districts having superintendents are Wheeling, Huntington, Parkersburg, Martinsburg and Charleston.

WEST VIRGINIA UNIVERSITY.

76. "The Agricultural College of West Virginia," Agricultural College of West Virginia. located and established at Morgantown, in the county of Monongalia, in pursuance to the act passed February seventh, one thousand eight hundred and sixty-seven, entitled "An act for the regulation of the West Virginia Agricultural College," shall be and remain as so established and located; and all the provisions of said act, except so far as the same may be altered by this chapter, shall remain in full force and effect to the same extent as if this chapter as amended had not been passed.

77. The name of said college shall hereafter be "The West Virginia University. West Virginia University," by which name it shall have and hold all the property, funds, investments, rights, powers and privileges, now had and held under the name prescribed in the above recited act.

78. For the government and control of said University there shall be a board of regents consisting of nine Regents of West Virginia University. persons, to be called "The Regents of the West Virginia University." As such board they may sue and be sued, and have a common seal. The said board shall have the custody and control of the property and funds of said University, except as otherwise provided by law. They shall have the power to accept from any person or persons any gift, grant or devise of money, land or other property intended for the use of the University, and shall by such acceptance, be trustees of the funds and property which may come into the possession or

under the control of said board by such gift, grant or
devise, and shall invest and hold such funds and property, and apply the proceeds and property in such manner as the donor may prescribe by the terms of his gift,
grant or devise, and shall invest and hold such funds and
property and apply the proceeds and property in such
manner as the donor may prescribe by the terms of the
gift, grant or devise.

Quorum. A majority of said regents shall constitute a quorum
for the transaction of business, except that for making
arrangements for the erection of buildings, or the permanent alteration thereof, or the appointment to, or removal from office of professors, or fixing their compensation or changing any rule or regulation adopted by a
majority of the board, in which case all of the regents
shall be notified in writing by the secretary of the
board, of the time, place and object of the meeting proposed to be held for any of the purposes excepted in
this section; and the concurrence of a majority of the
regents shall be required.

Regents; when appointed. The said board of regents shall be appointed by the
Governor on or before the first day of June, in the year
one thousand eight hundred and ninety-seven and on or
after the tenth day of March in the year one thousand
eight hundred and ninety-seven, as follows: three shall
be designated to serve for two years, three for four
years, and three for six years, from the first day of
June, in the year one thousand eight hundred and ninety-
seven, and before the expiration of said respective
terms he shall appoint between the tenth day of March
Governor to appoint regents. and the first day of June, in each year in which said respective terms shall expire, three regents to serve for
the full term of six years, from the first day of June
of the year in which said appointments shall be made,
but not more than two regents in any one class, nor
more than five in all shall be members of the same political party or organization, and not more than one shall
be appointed from any senatorial district of the State.

Governor to fill vacancies. The Governor shall nominate for the approval of the
Senate, the nine regents herein provided for, and in the
year one thousand eight hundred and ninety-nine, and
every second year thereafter, he shall nominate, and by
and with the advice and consent of the Senate, appoint
three regents in the place of the class whose terms shall expire in said year.   The Governor may in like manner,
fill any vacancy that may occur in said board; and any
one appointed a regent by him during the recess of the
Senate shall be a regent until the next session of the

Senate thereafter; and the terms of office of the present board of regents shall expire on the thirtieth day of May, in the year one thousand eight hundred and ninety-seven.

79. The board of regents shall from time to time establish such departments of education in literature, science, art, agriculture and military tactics as they may deem expedient, and as the funds under their control may warrant, and purchase such materials, implements and apparatus, as may be requisite to proper instruction in all said branches of learning, so as to carry out the spirit of the act of Congress aforesaid, approved July second, one thousand eight hundred and sixty-two. *Courses of study.*

80. The said board shall establish and declare such rules and regulations and by-laws not inconsistent with the laws of this State, or the United States, as they may deem necessary for the proper organization, the tuition of students and good government of said University and the protection of public property belonging thereto. They shall appoint a superintendent of the buildings and grounds, a secretary for said board and also a treasurer, who shall be members of the faculty of the University, and shall not receive any compensation for services as such superintendent, secretary and treasurer. No salary shall be paid to the secretary of the executive committee. From the said treasurer they shall take a bond with ample security, and conditioned according to law, for the faithful keeping and disbursing such money as is herein, or may be hereafter appropriated, and such other money as may be allowed by said board to come into his hands from time to time; they shall also settle with him annually or oftener if they think best; inspect annually all the property belonging to said University and make a full report of the condition, income, expenditures and management of said University, annually, to the Governor; to be by him laid before the Legislature. *Rules and regulations.* *Officers of the University.*

81. The board shall have power to create a preparatory department to said University, and establish any other professorships than those indicated heretofore, if the same be deemed essential; to fix the salaries of the several professors, and to remove them for good cause, but in case of removal the concurrence of a majority of the regents shall be required, and the reasons for a removal shall be communicated in a written statement to the Governor. *Preparatory department.*

82. Besides prescribing the general terms upon which students may be admitted, and the course of instruction, the regents are still further empowered to admit as regular students or cadets of said university not more than *Appointment of cadets.*

one hundred and forty-four students, of whom each regent may appoint not more than sixteen who are not less than sixteen years of age nor more than twenty-one, whose term of service shall not be less than two nor more than five years, which appointment shall be made upon undoubted evidence of good moral character and sound physical condition, but not more than twelve cadets shall be appointed from any senatorial district and not more than five from any one county.

Cadets have free books,etc. 83. The cadets admitted under the provisions of the preceding section shall be entitled to all the privileges, immunities, educational advantages, and benefits of the University, free of charge for admission, tuition, books and stationery, and shall constitute the public guard of the University, and of the public property belonging thereto; and of the ordinance and ordinance stores, and camp and garrison equipage, of which a sufficient supply shall be kept in the arsenal belonging to the institution. And the professors and the students of the University receiving instruction in military tactics and the art of war, shall be individually and collectively responsible for the preservation and safe-keeping of all arms and camp equipage belonging to said institution.

Expenses of regents. 84. All reasonable expenses incurred by said regents in discharging the duties hereby imposed upon them (not, however, including wages or *per diem* compensation) shall be allowed by the Governor and paid out of the treasury of the State, in like manner as other sums are drawn therefrom: *Provided, however*, That such expenditure shall not exceed five hundred dollars per annum.

Graduation. 85. The president, board of regents and faculty may graduate any student of the university found (after proper examination) duly qualified, and shall certify the same by affixing the seal of the University to his diploma.

Investment of land funds. 86. The fund derived from the sale of United States land warrants which have been donated to this State for the purpose of endowing an agricultural college, shall be invested by the Governor in a loan of public stock of the United States, or otherwise, as required by Congress, for the use and benefit of the said University.

AGRICULTURAL EXPERIMENT STATION.

Agricultural Experiment Station. [86a. WHEREAS, The Congress of the United States has in its widom seen fit to appropriate the sum of fifteen thousand dollars annually for the establishment and maintenance of an agricultural experiment station in this state, to aid in acquiring and diffusing among the people

useful and practical information on the subjects connected with agriculture, and to promote scientific inves-
tigation and experiment respecting the principles and
applications of agricultural science, to be established in
connection with and under the direction of the college
of this State, established in accordance with the provisions of an act approved July 2, 1862, entitled, "An act
donating public lands to the several States and Terri-
tories which may provide colleges for the benefit of agriculture and the mechanic arts," and,

WHEREAS, The West Virginia University by an act
of the Legislature of West Virginia, entitled, "An act,
for the regulation of the West Virginia Agricultural
College," passed February 7, 1867, and other acts of the
Legislature amendatory, thereof, is the institution of
this State receiving the benefits of the above mentioned
land grant fund; and,

WHEREAS, In accordance with the provisions of section 9 of aforementioned act of Congress establishing
said experiment stations, the Governor of West Virginia
has accepted for the West Virginia University the congressional appropriation for the establishment of an
agricultural experiment station, and

WHEREAS, The board of regents of the West Virginia
University, in accordance with section 1, of the afore-
named congressional act, approved March 2, 1887, has
established a department in the West Virginia University, known as "the West Virginia Agricultural
Experiment Station," which is now in full working
order and issuing regular bulletins for the diffusion of
information among the people of the State, as required
by law; and which is now well and thoroughly equip-
ped with chemical laboratories, apparatus and ma-
chinery, and has a staff of scientific men employed and
carrying on the work contemplated in the congressional
act, therefore,

Be it enacted by the Legislature of West Virginia.

1. That the State of West Virginia hereby assents to
and accepts from the government of the United States
the grants of money authorized by said act of congress,
and assents to the purposes of said grants. *State accepts government grants.*

II. The bulletins and annual reports required to be
published under section four of said act, shall be
printed at the expense of the State, by the State printer,
in such editions or numbers as the mailing list of the experiment station shall indicate as being required, and
shall be distributed by the station free of all charge to
farmers and other citizens of the State desiring the
same. *Bulletins.*

State Normal School.

87. The "West Virginia State Normal School," established under and by virtue of the act passed February twenty-seventh, one thousand eight hundred and sixty-seven, entitled "An act for the establishment of a State Normal School," shall be and remain at Marshall College, in the county of Cabell, as provided in said act, and all the provisions of said act, and of all other acts in relation thereto, shall be, and remain in full force, except so far as the same may be altered by this chapter.

Regents.

For the government and control of said school and its branches, there shall be a board of regents, consisting of the State Superintendent of Free Schools, together with one person from each congressional district in the State, to be appointed by the Governor, as hereinafter provided, who shall be called the "Regents of the State Normal School," and as such may have a common seal, sue, and be sued, plead and be impleaded, contract and be contracted with, and take, hold and possess

Transfer of property.

real and personal estate for the use of said school. The transfer and conveyance by the board of supervisors of Cabell county of the lands and buildings of Marshall College, and of the real estate heretofore conveyed by the Central Land Company of West Virginia to the regents of said school heretofore appointed, is hereby accepted, confirmed and legalized. But in case the said school should at any time hereafter be removed from the said Marshall College, the said property so conveyed shall revert to and be vested in the county court for the use of said county of Cabell. The said board of regents shall be appointed by the Governor, and equally divided between the two dominant political parties, on or before the first day of June, one thousand eight hundred and ninety-five, one of whom shall serve one year, one two years, one three years and one four years, and upon the expiration of said term of service he shall appoint one for the full term of four years as hereinbefore provided.

Rules and regulations.

88. The said school shall be under the general supervision and control of the said regents. They shall have full power and authority to adopt and establish such by-laws, rules and regulations for its government as they may deem necessary and proper, to effect the object of its establishment, not inconsistent with the laws of this state. They shall fix the number and compensation of the teachers, and others to be employed therein, and appoint and remove the same; prescribe the preliminary examination of pupils, and the terms and conditions on which they shall be received and instructed in said school: *Provided*, That all pupils admitted free of tuition to any one school, shall not exceed in number the

whole number appointed to such county for admission Number of pupils. to all normal schools of the State; the branches of learning to be taught in each department thereof; and shall determine the number of pupils to be received in the normal department of said school from each county or judicial circuit of this State, conforming as nearly as possible to the ratio of population therein, and the mode of selecting them. The pupils admitted into the normal department of said school shall be admitted to all the privileges thereof, free from all charges of tuition, or for use of books or apparatus; that every such pupil shall pay for all books lost by him or any damage done by him to such books or apparatus; and any pupil in said school may be dismissed therefrom by said regents, or by the executive committee, subject to the approval of the regents, for immoral or disorderly conduct, or for neglect or inability to perform his duty. The State Superintendent of Free Schools shall prepare suit- Diplomas. able diplomas to be granted to the students of the normal department of said school who have completed the course of study and discipline prescribed by said regents. The said regents may establish a pay department in said school whenever the accommodations thereof will admit of the same, and may admit into such department so many paying students as can be accommodated therein from this or any other State, whether they desire to become teachers of schools or not.

They may cause to be taught in the said department of said school, all or any of the branches of learning usually taught in colleges and seminaries, and for that purpose may establish therein the necessary professorships.

They may also make all the necessary rules and regu- Tuition, etc. lations for the government of said department and prescribe the tuition and the terms of admission therein. The said school shall continue to be called and known by the name of "Marshall College."

CXLII. The number of persons who may receive appointments to the normal schools of the State is one thousand, divided among the counties according to population

CXLIII. It is the practice to allow persons attending either of the State Normal Schools, under appointment, to teach one term of school each year if desired, and yet hold the appointment. The same rule is held to be good in case of colored teachers attending the West Virginia Colored Institute.

CXLIV. Clearly under section 88 of the school law, two departments are contemplated. One known as the normal department, and the other as the pay or academic department. It is intended that in the latter department, persons are admitted who do not desire to take the normal course, or if they have taken the normal course, who desire to pursue a higher grade of studies. I see nothing to prevent those who have taken the normal course, and have graduated from reviewing the studies contained in the normal course, free of charge.

The purpose of the normal course is to prepare teachers, and a reviewing of that course would be to make the teachers more perfect.—*T. S. Riley, Attorney-General.*

Executive Committee

89. The said regents shall appoint three intelligent and discreet persons, residents of the county of Cabell, who shall constitute an executive committee for the care and immediate management and control of said school, subject to the rules and regulations prescribed by the regents. Said committee shall (subject to the control of said regents), designate the person to take charge of the boarding department of said school, and fix the price to be paid for board therein. They shall from time to time make full and detailed reports to said regents of the condition, working and prospects of said school, and shall perform such other duties in relation thereto as the said regents may from time to time prescribe.

Fairmont branch.

90. The branch of the state normal school established at Fairmont, under and in pursuance of the act passed March fourth, one thousand eight hundred and sixty-eight, entitled, "An act providing for the purchase of the West Virginia Normal School at Fairmont," shall be and remain at that place, and all provisions of said act shall remain in full force, except so far as the same may be altered by this chapter. Said school shall be under the jurisdiction and control of the regents of the state normal school, in the same manner and to the same extent as the state normal school at Marshall College.

West Liberty branch.

91. The branch of the state normal school established at West Liberty, under and in pursuance of the act passed March first, one thousand eight hundred and seventy, entitled "An act to establish a branch normal school at West Liberty, in Ohio county," shall be and remain at that place, and all the provisions of said act shall remain in full force, except so far as the same may be altered by this chapter. Said school shall be under the jurisdiction and control of the regents of the state normal school, in the same manner and to the same extent as the state normal school at Marshall College.

Glenville branch.

92. The branch of the State normal school established at Glenville, under and in pursuance of the act passed the nineteenth day of February, one thousand eight hundred and seventy-two, entitled "an act to establish a branch normal school at Glenville, Gilmer county," shall be and remain at that place, and all the provisions of said act shall remain in full force, except so far as the same may be altered by this chapter. Said school shall be under the jurisdiction and control of the regents of the State normal school, in the same manner and to the same extent as the State normal school at Marshall College.

Shepherdstown branch.

93. The branch of the State normal school established at Shepherdstown, under and in pursuance of the act

passed and approved February fourteenth, one thousand eight hundred and seventy-two, entitled "an act to establish a brance normal school at Shepherdstown, in the county of Jefferson," shall be and remain at that place, and all the provisions of said act shall remain in full force, except so far as the same may be altered by this chapter. Said school shall be under the jurisdiction and control of the regents of the State normal school, in the same manner and to the same extent as the State normal school at Marshall College.

94. The branch of the State normal school at *Concord, in Mercer county, established by the act passed the twenty-eighth day of February, one thousand eight hundred and seventy-two, entitled "an act to locate a branch State normal school at Concord, in the county of Mercer, shall be and remain at that place, and all the provisions of said act shall remain in full force, except so far as the same may be altered by this chapter. Said school shall be under the jurisdiction and control of the regents of the State normal school in the same manner and to the same extent as the State normal school at Marshall College.

Concord branch.

95. The principals of the State Normal school and its branches shall make, at the close of each term thereof, to the president of the board of regents, in addition to the annual reports required of them, a report, under oath, of the number of non-paying normal school pupils and the number of paying pupils in the several departments of the school in actual monthly attendance during said term.

Principal's reports.

96. The president of the board of regents of the State Normal School and its branches, upon receipt of the reports required in the ninety-fifth section of this chapter, shall furnish the Auditor of the State with the number of the non-paying Normal pupils in actual monthly attendance in each of the said Normal Schools, and the number of months of actual attendance, upon the receipt of which report, and upon the requisition of the president of the board of regents, the said auditor shall issue to the executive committee of each of said schools, warrants upon the treasury of the State for the amount due said schools, at the rate of three dollars and fifty cents per month for every non-paying Normal pupil reported as in monthly attendance.

A sum not to exceed thirty-two hundred dollars each year is hereby appropriated for each of the Normal Schools, payable out of the treasury of the State.

Appropriation.

The State Superintendent of Free Schools shall, if possible, in every year, make arrangements with some

---

*The name of the postoffice has been changed to Athens.

Colored teachers.

suitable institution of learning in this State for the education and Normal school-training of a number of colored teachers, in the proportion to the colored population of the State which the non-paying white students in the Normal Schools bear to the white population of the State; but the amount to be paid for each of said colored teachers shall not exceed the sum herein specified for each non-paying white student; and an additional sum to the extent necessary to pay the tuition of said colored students, is hereby appropriated, payable out of the treasury of the State in each year, as provided for in the next section, upon the requisition of the State Superintendent of Free Schools.

CXLV. "'Actual monthly attendance' of a non-paying pupil during any month of a school term, may be an attendance *bona fide* for a portion of the month. Sickness might prevent constant attendance during any month, yet if the pupil was in attendance in good faith during part of the month, when able to attend, the school would be entitled to $3.50 for such pupil for that month. * * The words 'actual monthly attendance' are used in the statute, so as to plainly prohibit pay being drawn for constructive monthly attendance."

"The attendance of the pupil must have commenced in a month and in good faith, with an intention of continuing. If the pupil does not attend at all during any month * * the law prohibits any pay being given."—*Alfred Caldwell, Attorney-General.*

Unearned appropriation.

97. If any normal school does not earn the amount of its annual appropriation of three thousand dollars, as aforesaid, in any year, the board of regents of the State Normal School and its branches are hereby authorized to expend in their discretion the unearned amount of its annual appropriation in the payment of teachers in another or others of such schools; and the auditor shall issue his warrants for such expenditures on the order of said board.

CXLVI. Section 96 as amended by chapter 45, Acts 1895, provides for an appropriation of thirty-two hundred dollars for each normal school.

Dealing with students.

98. I. If any money be lent or advanced, or anything be sold or let to hire, on credit to or for the use of any student or pupil under twenty-one years of age, at the West Virginia University, the West Virginia State Normal School or any of its branches, or any incorporated college in the State, without the previous permission, in writing, of his or her parent or guardian, or the president or principal of such institution, nothing shall be recovered therefor, and there shall, moreover, be forfeited to the State, by the person giving such credit, twenty dollars, and the amount or value of such thing. When such selling, letting, lending or advancing is by an agent, such forfeiture shall be by his principal, unless the principal shall within ten days after he has knowledge or information of the selling, letting, lending or advancing, give notice, in writing, of the

date, nature and amount thereof to the president or other head of the institution, in which case the forfeiture shall be by the agent.

II. All acts and parts of acts coming within the purview of this chapter, and inconsistent therewith, are hereby repealed.

Acts repealed.

THE WEST VIRGINIA SCHOOLS FOR THE DEAF AND BLIND.

[98*a*. I. That the name of the West Virginia Institution for the Deaf, Dumb and Blind be and the same is hereby changed to that of "The West Virginia Schools for the Deaf and the Blind."

Name.

The board of regents for the West Virginia Schools for the Deaf and Blind, shall be composed of nine members, whose term of office shall commence on the first day of June, one thousand eight hundred and ninety-seven.

Board of regents.

The Governor shall on the tenth day of March, one thousand eight hundred and ninety-seven, or as soon thereafter as convenient, nominate, and by and with the advice and consent of the Senate, appoint said nine regents for said schools, but said regents shall be divided into three classes of equal numbers and not more than two regents in each class shall belong to the same political party. Not more than one regent for the West Virginia Scools for the Deaf and the Blind shall be appointed from any one county.

Governor to appoint regents.

The term of office of the first-class shall be two years, of the second-class four years, and of the third-class six years.

On the tenth day of March, one thousand eight hundred and ninety-nine, or as soon thereafter as convenient, and every second year thereafter, the Governor shall nominate, and by and with the advice and consent of the Senate, appoint three regents for said schools, in place of the class whose term expires in said year; and the term of such regents shall commence on the first day of April in the year of their appointment and continue six years. The Governor may in like manner appoint regents to fill any vacancy that may occur in the board of said schools, and any one appointed a regent by him during the recess of the Senate, shall be a regent until the next session of the Senate thereafter.

Governor to fill vacancies.

Said members shall constitute collectively a body corporate with powers to rent, purchase and convey real estate, and with all other powers necessary for the carrying on of the institution for the education of the deaf and blind youth of West Virginia, established under the act passed March third, eighteen hundred and seventy, and to be known as "The Board of Regents of the West Virginia Schools for the Deaf and the Blind." Said board shall appoint one of their number as president, and in case of his absence a president *pro tem.* shall appoint a secretary, and all orders, drafts or requisitions for money from the State shall be signed by their secretary and countersigned by the president. Said board shall meet as hereinafter provided, and shall hold such other meetings as they may think necessary. Extra meetings may be called by the president or by any four members of the board by notifying the other members of the time and place of the meeting and of the nature of the business which renders an extra meeting necessary. A **Quorum.** majority of the board shall constitute a quorum for the transaction of all ordinary business, but the board may, in its discretion, designate business of a nature to be specified by it, which may be transacted by a stated number of regents less than a quorum.

Principal. II. It shall be the duty of the principal under the direction of the board to superintend the affairs necessary for the proper conduct of the institution, and to make such general regulations as may be necessary for the successful management of the same, and to purchase such books and apparatus as may be necessary for the efficient working of the institution.

Teachers. III. Said board shall appoint all necessary teachers **Furniture.** and assistants, and shall provide the furniture, fixtures, apparatus and other things necessary for the comfort and convenience of inmates of the institution.

Steward. IV. The said board may, when they deem it necessary, elect a steward; and the principal and matron shall reside in the institution, and the steward and teacher in or **Salaries.** near it. All salaries shall be fixed by the board of regents, and shall be paid monthly or quarterly, as the board may deem proper, out of the fund appropriated by the legislature.

Visiting V. The board of regents shall employ as visiting phy- **physician.** sician of the institution, a physician of reputable standing in his profession, and it shall be his duty to render all medical assistance necessary to its inmates, and fix his salary, not to exceed three hundred dollars, to be paid in the same manner as a teacher.

Bond. VI. The principal and steward shall give bond with approved security in such amount as the board of regents may direct, for the faithful discharge of their respectives duties.

Rules and VII. The board of regents shall prescribe such by- **regulations.** laws, rules and regulations for the government and conduct of the institution under their charge as shall secure the harmonious and efficent management of said institu tion in all its parts. They shall require such reports from the principal, steward, matron and physician as in their opinion the institution may demand, and they shall annually, on or before the first day of December, report to the Governor all the facts and circumstances in connection with the conduct and progress of the institution, with a careful statement of all the receipts and disbursements of the same, and shall accompany their annual report with such recommendations and suggestions as will enable the State efficiently to foster and promote the enterprise of educating the deaf, dumb and blind youth within its limits. The fiscal year of the institu- Fiscal year. tion shall end on the last day of September, and the accounts of the institution shall be kept with reference to said fiscal year; and there shall be an annual meeting of said board on the third Thursday in October in each and every year.

VIII. The board of regents may provide in said insti- Admission of tution accommodation for all the officers, assistants and pupils. employees, and for all the deaf, dumb and blind youth resident of the State of West Virginia who may apply for admission to the said institution, between the ages of eight and twenty-five years, and for such other deaf, dumb and blind persons as may apply for admission as paying pupils, under such regulations as said board may direct, but all youth admitted must be of sound mind and not afflicted with any contagious or offensive disease.

IX. All such deaf, dumb and blind youth residents Admission of of the State of West Virginia between the ages of eight pupils. and twenty-five years, shall be admitted to pupilage in the institution on application to the principal; until the institution is filled, applicants shall be admitted in the order of their application, and it shall be the duty of the principal to keep a careful record of the names of all pupils admitted with the dates of their admission and discharge, their age, postoffice address, the name of their parents or guardians, the degree, cause and circumstances of their deafness or blindness.

All such deaf, dumb and blind pupils shall be ad- Charges. mitted as above directed without charge for board and tuition; and when not otherwise provided with clothing they shall be furnished by the institution while they are pupils in the same, and the principal shall make out an account therefor in each case against the respective counties from which said pupils are sent, in an amount not exceeding forty dollars per annum for every such pupil, which account shall be certified by the principal and countersigned by the secretary, and which shall be transmitted by the principal to the Auditor of the State, whose duty it shall be to transmit a

copy of the same to the clerks of the county courts of
the respective counties against which they are; and the
Duty of county officers. county court of such counties shall thereupon at their
next sessions, respectively, thereafter held for the pur-
pose of making a county levy, include in such levy the
amount of said accounts against their counties, respectively, and cause an order to issue on the sheriff of the
county in favor of the Auditor of the State, and cause
the same to be transmitted by the clerk of said court to
the Auditor, whose duty it shall be to collect the same
and place it to the credit of the institution, to be drawn
out upon requisition as a part of the current expenses
of said schools.   If the same is not paid to the Auditor
by the respective counties from which they are due in
a reasonable time it shall be the duty of the Auditor to
collect the same by law.

Term of pupilage. The term of pupilage shall be five years at least, and
for so much longer term as in the discretion of the
board and principal their condition and progress would
seem to justify.   After all the applicants between the
prescribed ages of eight and twety five years have been
admitted, if there is still room, the principal may admit other deaf and dumb and blind persons upon application who may be of suitable age to receive any advantage of the institution, and upon such terms as the
board may prescribe; but it shall be distinctly understood that such persons shall withdraw from the institution in the order of the dates of their admission to make
room for new applicants between the ages herein
already prescribed.

Course of instruction. X. The course of instruction in the institution shall
be prescribed by the board of regents with the advice
of the principal, and shall be as extensive both in the
intellectual, musical and mechanical departments, as the
capacities and interests of the pupils may require.

Assessors' registration. XI. In addition to their other duties the assessors of
the State are hereby required to register in a book, to
be furnished them by the Auditor for the purpose, the
name of all the deaf and the blind persons in their
respective districts, with the degree and cause of deafness and blindness in each case as far as can be ascertained from the heads of families, or from other persons
whom the assessors may conveniently consult, their ages,
the names of their parents or guardians, their post-office
address, and such other circumstances as may constitute
useful statistical information in making the said institution promptly efficient in ameliorating the condition of
the deaf and the blind by education. They shall complete the registration as early as possible, in the first
annual assessment after the passage of this act, and shall

forward their report directly to the auditor, who shall if practicable before the first day of July, or as soon thereafter as possible, make an alphabetical abstract of all the facts furnished him by the assessors' reports, and shall send the same by mail to the principal of the West Virginia schools for the deaf and the blind, and said principal is hereby further required to put himself in immediate correspondence with all the deaf and blind persons, of suitable age and condition, mentioned in the auditor's abstract, with a view to their admission as pupils into the West Virginia schools for the deaf and the blind. *Principal to correspond with persons named on registration list.*

The assessors shall receive for the extra duties hereby imposed, the same compensation as is now allowed them for the registration of births and deaths, and shall be liable to the same penalties for failure to discharge these duties.]

THE WEST VIRGINIA COLORED INSTITUTE.

98*b*. An act accepting the provisions of the act of Congress, approved August thirtieth, eighteen hundred and ninety, entitled "An act to apply a portion of the proceeds of the public lands to the more complete endowment and support of the colleges for the benefit of agriculture and the mechanic arts, established under the provisions of an act of Congress, approved July second, eighteen hundred and sixty-two," and providing for the apportionment of said endowment according to the provisions of said act.

WHEREAS, The Congress of the United States of America, by an act approved August thirtieth, eighteen hundred and ninety, entitled, "An act to apply a portion of the proceeds of the public lands to the more complete endowment and support of the colleges for the benefit of agriculture and the mechanic arts, established under the provisions of an act of Congress approved July second, eighteen hundred and sixty-two," made an appropriation to each state and territory of fifteen thousand dollars for the year ending June thirtieth, eighteen hundred and ninety; and an annual increase of said appropriation thereafter for ten years by the additional sum of one thousand dollars over the preceding year, after which time the annual amount so appropriated will be twenty-five thousand dollars, for the more complete endowment and maintenance of the colleges established under the act of Congress last aforesaid, "to be applied only to instruction in agriculture, the mechanic arts, the English language, and the various branches of mathematical, physical, natural and economic science, with special reference to their application in the industries of life; and to the facilities for such instruction," and

WHEREAS, By a proviso in said act no State can obtain the benefits thereof, where facilities are not provided for the instruction of colored students in said branches of study, either in the same institution or in separate institutions, and the legislatures of the several states are required to make an equitable division of said annual appropriation where such separate institutions are provided, and report the same to the Secretary of the Interior, and

WHEREAS, The Constitution of the State of West Virginia forbids the education of white and colored youths in the same State schools, and this State having heretofore made no provision for the separate education of colored youth in agricultural and the mechanic arts; and the enumeration of the white and colored youths of this State, of school age, being about 250,000 white and 12,000 colored, it being the duty of this State to indicate a reasonable proportion of said appropriations to be set apart annually for the instruction of the colored youth of the State, the sum of $3,000 is hereby indicated as an equitable portion of said appropriations for five years from the date of the passage of this act, and after that time $5,000 as long as such appropriation continues; and

WHEREAS, By the terms of the said act of Congress of the United States, approved August thirtieth, eighteen hundred and ninety, it is necessary, in order to enable this State to share in the appropriations so made and to be made under the provisions of said last recited act, for the legislature to accept of the provisions of said act for and on behalf of this State, and to make proper and suitable provisions for said act upon which this State will be entitled to her distributable share of said appropriations, and to designate the institutions of learning to become the beneficiaries of said appropriations, and the officer of this State to whom the money shall be paid by the United States for the use of said beneficiaries. Therefore,

Be it enacted by the Legislature of West Virginia:

I. The Legislature of the State of West Virginia hereby accepts for said State, the terms and provisions of the said act of the Congress of the United States approved August thirtieth, eighteen hundred and ninety, for the objects and purposes mentioned and declared therein, and designates "The West Virginia University," established in pursuance of the Act of the Congress of the United States passed July 2, 1862, and a subsequent act passed by said Congress on April

Acceptance of Congressional grant.

19, 1864, at Morgantown, in the county of Monongalia in this State, as the beneficiary of said appropriation for the instruction of white students, and an institution to be located and provided for the purpose as hereinafter required and directed in the county of Kanawha, to be called "The West Virginia Colored Institute," for the beneficiary of said appropriation for the instruction of colored students to be paid to each in the proportion mentioned in the preamble to this act. And the said institution by the name of "The West Virginia Colored Institute," shall have and hold all the property, funds, rights, powers and privileges hereinafter mentioned.

II. For the government and control of said institute *Regents.* there shall be a board of regents consisting of five competent, intelligent and discreet persons, not more than three of whom shall belong to the same political party, appointed, from time to time as occasion may require, by the Governor, to be called the "Regents of of the West Virginia Colored Institute," and as such board they may sue and be sued, plead and be impleaded, and have a common seal. They shall have care, custody and control of the property and funds of the institute, and may accept from any person or persons, gifts of money, or property, for the use of said institute, and all such money and property when so received by them shall be held in trust by them for the use and benefit of the institute, and applied thereto as the donors may have directed, and if no such direction have been given, as a majority of the regents may determine.

III. The board of regents shall from time to time estab-*Regents to to establish departments.* lish such departments of education in literature, science, art and agriculture, not inconsistent with the terms of the several acts of Congress hereinbefore referred to as they deem expedient, and as the funds under their control will warrant, and purchase such materials, implements, and apparatus as may be requisite to the proper instruction of said colored students in all said branches of learning as to carry out the intent and purposes of said acts of Congress.

IV. The said board shall establish and declare such *Rules and regulations.* rules, regulations and by-laws, not inconsistent with the laws of the United States or of this State, as they may deem necessary for the proper organization, the tuition of the students and the good government of the institute, and the protection of the property belonging thereto. All reasonable expenses incurred by said regents in the discharge of their duties hereby imposed upon them shall be allowed by the Governor and paid

out of the treasury of the State, in like manner as other
charges on the treasury are paid.

State Treasurer to receive grants. V. The Treasurer of this State is hereby designated
as the officer to receive from the Secretary of the Treasury of the United States the said several sums of money
so to be paid to this State aforesaid, for the uses and
purposes aforesaid. He shall keep an exact account of
the moneys so received, and shall place to the credit of
each of said benificiaries thereof, its due proportion of
the same. The sums so placed to the credit of the West
Virginia University shall be paid out by him on the orders of the board of regents thereof, and the sums so
placed to the credit of the West Virginia Colored Institute, shall be paid out by him on the orders of the board
of regents of said institute. And said treasurer shall
include in his biennial report to the Governor a statement of his receipts and disbursements under the provisions of this act.

Site and buildings. VI. It shall be the duty of the board of the school
fund to proceed with all reasonable dispatch to procure
the necessary quantity of farming land not exceeding
fifty acres in all in some suitable and proper locality in
the county of Kanawha, with a title thereto clear and
unquestionable, and to erect the necessary buildings and
make the necessary improvements thereon, for the purposes of this act, and to comply in good faith with the
terms and conditions, and to carry into effect the objects
and purposes of the acts of Congress in making said
appropriations.

Ten thousand dollars to carry out this act. VII. And in order to enable said board to perform
the duties required of them by this act, the sum of ten
thousand dollars is hereby appropropriated and placed
at their disposal, payable out of any money in the treasury not otherwise appropriated: *Provided*, That said
board may in their discretion borrow the said sum of
ten thousand dollars from the "school fund" mentioned
in section 4 of article XII of the Constitution of this
State, at six per cent. interest per annum, and execute the
bonds of the State therefor, payable with interest as
aforesaid, not more than ten years from the date thereof.

WEST VIRGINIA REFORM SCHOOL.

Reform School. |98e. I. An institution to be called "The West Virginia Reform School," is hereby established, and shall
hereafter be carried on in a suitable building or buildings for the purpose, to be erected by the State at such
locality as may be selected in accordance with this act.
This institution shall be under the control of a board of
directors hereinafter provided for.

II. The board of directors shall be composed of six Board of members, and not more than four of them of the same directors. political party.

The Governor shall, on the tenth day of March, eighteen hundred and ninety-seven, or as soon thereafter as convenient, nominate and by and with the advice and consent of the Senate, appoint said six directors for said school, whose term of office shall commence on the first day of June, one thousand eight hundred and ninety-seven. Said directors shall be divided into three classes of equal numbers, and not more than one director shall be appointed from any one county. The term of office of the first class shall be two years, of the second class four years, and of the third class six years.

On the tenth day of March, one thousand eight hun- When dred and ninety-nine, or as soon thereafter as conven- appointed. ient, and every second year thereafter the Governor shall nominate, and by and with the advice and consent of the Senate, appoint two directors for said school, in place of the class whose term expires in said year. And the term of said directors shall commence on the first day of April in the year of their appointment and continue six years.

The Governor may, in like manner, fill any vacancy Vacancies. that may occur in the board, and any one appointed a director by him during the recess of the Senate, shall hold office until the next session of the Senate thereafter.

III. The board of directors shall biennially choose one of their body to be president of the board, and in his President. absence shall choose a president *pro tempore*. A majority of the board shall constitute a quorum, but the board Quorum. may in its discretion designate business, of a nature by it to be specified, which may be transacted by a stated number of directors less than a quorum.

IV. The board of directors shall make such by-laws, Rules and ordinances, rules and regulations relative to the manage- regulations. ment, government, instrtruction, discipline, training, employment and disposition of the minors in the reform school, not contrary to law, as they may deem proper, and shall appoint such officers, agents and servants as they may deem necessary to transact the business and carry on the operation of said reform school, and may designate their duties.

V. The board of directors shall make an annual re- Directors' port to the Governor of all their transactions, of the report. number of minors received by them into said reform school, the disposition which shall be made of such minors, by instructing or employing them therein or by binding them out as apprentices; the receipts and expenditures of said board of directors, and generally all such facts and particulars as may tend to exhibit the effect, whether beneficial or otherwise, of said reform school.

Manner of commitment. VI. The manner of receiving inmates into the West Virginia Reform School shall be in either of the following modes, namely:

First. Male minors under the age of sixteen years may be committed by a justice of the peace of any of the counties in the State, on complaint and due proof made to him by the parent, guardian or next friend of such minor, that by reason of incorrigible or vicious conduct, such minor has rendered his control beyond the power of such parent, guardian or next friend, and made it manifestly requisite that from regard for the morals and future welfare of such minor and the peace and order of society, he should be placed in the West Virginia Reform School.

Second. Male minors under the age of sixteen years may be committed by the authority aforesaid, when complaint and due proof have been made that such minor is a proper subject for said reform school by reason of vagrancy or of incorrigible or vicious conduct, and that from the moral depravity or otherwise of the parent, guardian or next friend, in whose custody such minor may be, such parent, guardian or next friend is incapable or unwilling to exercise proper care and discipline over such incorrigible or vicious minor.

Third. Such male minors under the age of sixteen years as their parents, guardian or next friend may desire to place therein for temporary restraint and discipline, where parents, guardian or next friend shall agree and contract with the board of directors for their support and maintenance.

And fourth. Male minors committed by the several courts of the State, as provided by section 7 of this chapter.

Male minors committed. VII. Whenever any male minor, under the age of sixteen years, shall be convicted in any of the courts of this State of a felony or of a misdemeanor, punishable by imprisonment, the judge of said court in his discretion, and with reference to the character of the reform school as a place of reform and not of punishment, instead of sentencing said minor to be confined in the penitentiary or county jail, may order him to be removed to and confined in the said reform school, to remain until he shall have arrived at the age of twenty-one years, unless sooner discharged or bound as an apprentice by the board of directors; but no such boy shall be retained in said school after the superintendent shall

have reported him, and he has been found by the board
or its executive committee, to be fully reformed. Male
minors under sixteen years of age, convicted in any of the
courts of the United States for the district of West Virginia, or of any offense punishable by imprisonment, may
also be received into said reform school upon such regulations, and such terms as to their maintenance and support, as may be prescribed by the board of directors,
and assented to by the proper authorities of the United
States. And in all cases, before any minor is transferred to said reform school, due notice shall be given
to the superintendent and an answer received from him
that there is room in the reform school for such minor.

VIII. It shall be the duty of the justice of the peace *Data to be annexed to commitment.*
when committing a minor to said reform school under
the first and second clauses of section six of this chapter, in addition to the commitment, to annex to said
commitment the names and residences of the different
witnesses examined before him, and the substance of
the testimony given by them respectively, on which the
adjudication was found.

IX. In all proceedings before justices of the peace for *Guardian ad litem.*
commitment of minors to the said reform school under
the first and second clauses of section six of this chapter, the justice shall appoint some discreet and disinter-
ested person guardian *ad litem* for such minor, whose
duty it shall be to represent the interest of said minor
and see that no injustice is done him; and the guardian
ad litem of said minor shall have the right to demand a
jury of twelve men to try the truth of the charges
made against said minor, and said jury shall be selected
and said trial shall be conducted in the same manner as
is provided by law for the trial of criminal cases before
justices by juries. And said guardian *ad litem* or said
minor shall have the same right of appeal from any
final decision rendered against said minor in any such
proceedings, whether upon a trial by jury or otherwise,
as is allowed by law in other criminal cases tried before
justices.

X. The West Virginia Reform School shall be exclu- *Male inmates only.*
sively charged with the reformation and care of male
minors, but white and colored inmates shall be kept separate.

XI. The board of directors shall have power to bind *Children may be bound out as ap- prentices.*
out male children committed to their care, with the con-
sent of such children, as apprentices during their minor-
ity to such person and place, whether in or out of the
State, and to learn some proper trade and employment
as in the judgment of said board will be most conducive
to the reformation and future benefit and advantage of

such children, and the indentures by which said children shall be bound, shall contain the covenants and provisions prescribed by chapter eighty-one of the Code of West Virginia, relating to master and apprentices, and all the provisions of said chapter shall apply to apprentices bound under this section, so far as applicable.

Commission to select site. XII. A commission consisting of the State Superintendent of Free Schools, and one member from each Congressional district of the State to be appointed by the Governor, shall within four months after this act becomes in force as a law, select such locality as it may deem best as the site for the West Virginia Reform School, and procure a good title to such site, and report their action to the Governor as soon as such selection is made and the title procured. And as soon as practicable after said report is made to the Governor, the "board of directors" herein provided for, shall contract for and cause to be constructed on the said site, such building or buildings as may be needed in carrying out the provisions of this act. *Provided*, That the sum to be expended for said site and for constructing said building, shall at no time exceed the appropriation for said purpose.

Appropriation for site and buildings. XIII. The sum of five thousand dollars to be paid out of the State fund for the fiscal year ending September 30, 1889, and five thousand dollars to be paid out of the State fund for the fiscal year ending September 30, 1890, is hereby appropriated out of any money in the treasury not otherwise appropriated to be used in procuring said site for said Reform School, and in providing suitable buildings and accommodations for the same, and in carrying on said Reform School when established; and the reasonable expenses of the commissioners herein provided for, selecting a site for the said Reform School, shall be allowed and paid out of said money hereby appropriated.

Boys to remain until of age. XIV. Every boy sent to the reform school shall remain until he is twenty-one years of age, unless sooner discharged, or bound as an apprentice by the board of directors; but no boy shall be retained after he has been reported by the superintendent and found by the board or executive committee to be fully reformed.

Escaping boys to be returned, &c. XV. If any person shall entice or attempt to entice away from the reform school any boy legally committed to the same, or shall aid or abet any boy to escape from said reform school, or shall harbor, conceal, or aid in harboring or concealing any boy who shall have escaped therefrom, such person shall be deemed guilty of a misdemeanor, and, upon conviction thereof, shall be fined not less than ten nor more than one hundred dollars;

and the superintendent or any of his assistants, or any one authorized in writing by him, or any sheriff, constable, policeman or other peace officer, shall have power, and it is hereby made his duty, to arrest any boy, when in his power to do so, who shall have escaped from said school and return him thereto.

XVI. Justices and constables and juries shall have the same fees in the proceedings for the commitment of boys to the reform school as are allowed by law for similar services in other criminal cases, and such fees shall be audited by the county court of the county, and paid out of the county treasury. For transporting a boy to the reform school the officer having him in charge shall be allowed five cents for each mile of necessary travel, either in going or returning; and said costs of transportation in case the boy has been convicted of a felony shall be paid out of the State treasury in the same manner that other criminal charges are paid out of said treasury; and in case the boy has been convicted of a misdemeanor, or been committed by a justice, said costs of transportation shall be paid out of the treasury of the county, from which said boy is committed, in the same manner as other criminal charges are paid out of the treasuries of the counties. *Fees and charges.*

PREPARATORY BRANCH OF THE WEST VIRGINIA UNIVERSITY AT MONTGOMERY, FAYETTE COUNTY.

Be it enacted by the Legislature of West Virginia.

1. There shall be established a school at Montgomery, in the county of Fayette, to be called the Preparatory Branch of the West Virginia University, by which name it shall have and hold all the property, funds, investments, rights, powers and privileges granted by this act, by bequest, private subscriptions, donation or otherwise. *Name.*

2. It being estimated that the sum of ten thousand dollars will be needed for the purpose of the erection of suitable buildings and the purchase of a site for said school, therefore the sum of five thousand dollars payable out of the revenues of this fiscal year, one thousand eight hundred and ninety-five, is hereby appropriated out of any money in the treasury, to be expended under the directions of the board of regents of said school for said purpose. *Appropriation.*

For the government and control of said school there shall be a board of regents consisting of the state superintendent of free schools and the the members of the board of regents of the West Virginia University. As *Regents.*

such they may sue and be sued, plead and be impleaded, contract and be contracted with and have a common seal.

Powers of Regents. 3. Said board shall have all the powers to act and shall act and be controlled according to and under the laws of chapter forty-five of the code of West Virginia, governing the board of regents of the West Virginia University, except as herein limited by this act.

Board to let contract. 4. Said board of regents shall as soon as this act takes effect, let to contract and provide for the erection of suitable buildings upon the site selected and furnished for said school by the citizens of the town of Montgomery, Fayette county. Said buildings to be completed and said school opened not later than the first day of September, one thousand eight hundred and ninety-six. Said board shall provide suitable books, furniture and apparatus necessary for the successful operation of said school, all of which shall be paid for as herein provided.

Property vested in Board. 5. That the property in all grounds, buildings and improvements erected under the provisions of this act, shall be vested in the board of regents of said school, to be used and controlled, as in like manner, is the property of the West Virginia University used and controlled by its said board of regents.

Branches taught. 6. There shall be taught in said school such branches of learning as are taught in the preparatory department of the West Virginia University and in the normal schools of this State; but no student shall receive instructions free of tuition in any of the branches herein designated, except as to such as are taught free in the preparatory department of the University of West Virginia.

Teachers. 7. It shall be the duty of the said board of regents to employ and fix the salaries of a sufficient and competent corps of teachers and other necessary officers. Said teachers and officers to be paid as is provided by law for the payment of teachers and officers of the West Virginia University.

Tuition 8. All students of this or other States desiring to take other branches of study than those designated in said preparatory courses or take other course of study in said school shall pay such tuition as shall be hereinafter fixed by the faculty of said school.

Tuition, etc.; how applied. 9. All money arising from tuition, matriculation fees or otherwise coming into the hands of the treasurer of said school shall be used and applied to the payment of the teachers' salaries and other liabilities of said school.

BLUEFIELD COLORED INSTITUTE.

1. There shall be established a school at Bluefield, Name. county of Mercer, to be called "Bluefield Colored Institute," by which name it shall have and hold all the property, funds, investments, rights, powers and privileges created by this act, by bequest, private subscription, donation or otherwise.

2. It being estimated that the sum of eight thousand Appropriation. dollars will be needed for the purpose of the erection of suitable buildings, and the purchase of a site for said school, therefore the sum of eight thousand dollars is hereby appropriated for said purpose; five thousand dollars of which sum shall be payable out of the revenues of this fiscal year, one thousand eight hundred and ninety-five, and three thousand dollars out of the revenues of the fiscal year of one thousand eight hundred and ninety-six, to be expended under the direction of the board of regents to be appointed for said school for said purpose of this act.

For the government and control of said school there Board of shall be a board of regents consisting of the State Regents. Superintendent of Free Schools, together with four other members of said board, to be appointed by the Governor, by and with the consent of the Senate, one each from the several Congressional districts of this State, not more than two of whom shall belong to the same political party, which board shall be known as the "Board of Regents of the Bluefield Colored Institute," and shall be a corporation, and as such may sue and be sued, plead and be impleaded, contract and be contracted with, and have a common seal. The said regents shall be appointed by the Governor and shall serve during his pleasure, and their compensation shall be such a per diem and actual expenses as other similar boards of the State.

3. Said boards shall have all the powers to act, and Powers of shall act and be controlled according to and under the board. laws governing the board of regents of the normal schools of this State, except as here limited by this act.

4. The said board of regents shall, as soon as this act Provisions for takes effect, let to contract and provide for a suitable school. building upon the site selected for said school by the said board of regents, said building to be completed and said school opened not later than the first day of September, one thousand eight hundred and ninety-six. Said board shall provide suitable books, furniture and apparatus necessary for the operation of said school, all of which shall be paid for as hereinafter provided.

5. That the property and all grounds and improve-

Property.

ments erected under the provisions of this act, shall be vested in the board of regents of said school, to be used and controlled in like manner as the property of the normal school and branches is used and controlled by its said board of regents.

Branches to be taught.

6. There shall be taught in said school such branches of learning as are taught in the preparatory department of the West Virginia University and in the normal schools of this State, but no student shall receive instruction free of tuition in any of the branches here designated except as provided in section ninety-six of chapter forty-five of the Code of West Virginia, and as to such as are taught free in the preparatory department of the University of West Virginia.

Teachers and officers.

7. It shall be the duty of the said board of regents to employ and fix the salaries of a sufficient and competent corps of teachers and other necessary officers, such teachers and officers to be paid as is provided by law for the payment of teachers and officers of the normal schools of this State. The said salaries to be paid out of any moneys in the State treasury not otherwise apportioned.

Tuition.

8. All students of this State desiring to take other branches of studies than those designated in said preparatory course or taking other courses of study in said school, shall pay such tuition as shall hereafter be fixed by the faculty of said school.

Foreign students.

9. All students from other states shall be reqired to pay such tuition as shall be designated by the said board of regents

Money collected.

10. All money arising from tuition, matriculation fees or otherwise, coming into the hands of the treasurer of said school, shall be used and applied to the payment of teachers' salaries and other liabilities of said school.

APPENDIX.

ORDER OF PROCEEDINGS AT THE FIRST ANNUAL MEETING OF THE BOARD AFTER THEIR ELECTION.

[See Section 8.]

1. Appoint a secretary.

2. Appoint one trustee for each sub-district.

3. Determine the number of months the schools shall be taught in the district during the school year.

4. Determine the number of teachers that may be employed in the sub-districts, allowing at least one for each school house.

5. Fix the salaries of teachers according to the grade of certificate

6. Ascertain the average salary of teachers per month.

7. Ascertain the whole number of months to be taught in the district.

8. Determine the aggregate amount of money necessary to pay all the teachers.

9. Ascertain the unexpended balance of the teachers' fund in the hands of the sheriff, due the district from last year, after paying all salaries due teachers the preceding year.

10. Ascertain any other moneys available to the teachers' fund.

11. Deduct these amounts from the aggregate amount necessary to pay all the teachers.

12. Lay the district levy for teachers' fund, large enough to cover this amount, making proper allowances for exonerations, delinquencies and commissions.

The following examples will be convenient for reference in making levies for school purposes:

Number of teachers to be employed in the district.......	20
Number of months to be taught during the year.........	5
Whole number of months to be taught in the district.....	100
Average salary of teachers.............................	$30
Amount of money to pay all teachers..................	$3,000
Deduct amount on hand, including apportionment to the district from general school fund, say................	$1,100
Amount to be levied for teachers' fund................	$1,900

To find the average salaries of the teachers, fix the salaries according to grade, say:

For a No. 3 certificate................................	$25
For a No. 2 certificate................................	$35
For a No. 1 certificate................................	$45
Divide by the number of grades.....................	3)105
Average salary of teacher per month.................	$35

To ascertain the number of cents to be levied on every one hundred dollars' valuation of property in the district to raise $1,900 by taxation, suppose the whole valuation in the district to be $500,000.

RULE—Drop the cents, if any, and add four ciphers to the amount in dollars to be raised by the levy, and divide by the amount in dollars taxable property.

Example: 500,000)19,000,000(38 cents.
                15,000,000

                4,000,000
                4,000,000

Similar calculations should be made in relation to the Building Fund.

14. Determine the method and enter it on record, for calling special meetings of the board when necessary.

FORM NO. I.

FORM OF ORDERS TO BE ENTERED OF RECORD BY THE BOARD OF
EDUCATION.

OFFICE OF THE BOARD OF EDUCATION OF............ }
          DISTRICT, IN THE COUNTY OF............ }

At a meeting of the Board of Education held on the......day of ...., 18.., there were present, ... president, and......
and......, members of the board.

On motion of........, it is ordered that........ be, and he is hereby appointed Secretary of this Board.

On motion, it is ordered that the following named persons be appointed trustees in the following named sub-districts, for a term of three years, and until their successors are appointed and qualified:

Trustee for Sub-District No. 1.

. . . .

Trustee for Sub-District No. 2.

. . . .

On motion of . . . . . ., it is ordered that the salaries of teachers per month, for the school year, shall be as follows, according to the grade of their certificate: For grade No. 1, $. . . .; for grade No. 2, $. . . .; for grade No. 3, $. . . .

It is found by the board that in addition to the available funds now on hand, $. . . . will be necessary for the payment of teachers' salaries for the current year, and on motion of . . . . . ., it is ordered that a tax of . . . . cents on the one hundred dollars' valuation of the real estate and personal property of the district be levied for that purpose.

(A similar order should be entered in relation to the levy for Building Fund.)

On motion of . . . . . ., it is ordered that the president and secretary of this board be authorized to sign, in vacation, all proper orders for the payment of money out of the teachers' fund or the building fund, for the salaries of teachers employed and claims allowed by the board, and that they report the orders drawn on each fund, at the next meeting of this board.

The secretary of this board made a report this day for the several orders drawn by him and the president, on the teachers' fund and the building fund, respectivey, since the last meeting of the board, as follows: An order on the teachers' fund, in favor of . . . . . ., a teacher, for $. . . .; an order in favor of . . . . . ., a teacher, for $; also an order on the building fund, in favor of. . . ., for work done on . . . . . . school house, for $. . . .: and an order, in favor of . . . . . . for furnishing wood for . . . . . . school house, for $. . . . . .

On motion of . . . . . ., it is ordered that when in the opinion of the president or of the two commissioners it is deemed necessary, the president or secretary may call a special meeting of this board.

On motion the board does now adjourn.

. . . .
                                                President.

. . . .
                    Secretary.

FORM NO. II.

ORDER OF APPOINTMENT TO FILL A VACANCY IN THE BOARD OF TRUSTEES.

[To be entered in records of the board.]

There being a vacancy in the board of trustees in sub-district no. ....., in the district of ...., on motion of ...., it is ordered that........ be, and he is hereby appointed to fill said vacancy for the unexpired term, and till his successor shall be appointed and qualified.

NOTE—This order of appointment should be entered in the record book of the board of education at a regular meeting, and a copy of it signed by the secretary of the board served upon the appointee.

FORM NO. III.

APPOINTMENT OF A MEMBER OF THE BOARD OF EDUCATION TO FILL A VACANCY.

OFFICE OF COUNTY SUPERRINTENDENT, ⎫
OF THE COUNTY OF......... ⎬
...., West Virginia., ...18..

It having been made known to me that there is a vacancy in the board of education in ....district in my said county, I ...., county superintendent of said county, in pursuance of the authority vested in me by law, hereby appoint...... ....to fill the vacancy in said board for the unexpired term.

........................, *County Superintendent.*

FORM NO. IV.

OATH OF OFFICE.

State of West Virginia, County of.........to wit:

I,............, do solemnly swear (or affirm) that I will support the Constitution of the United States, and the Constitution of this State, and that I will faithfully discharge the duties of my office of............to the best of my skill and judgment. So help me God.

         A—— B——.

Sworn to and subscribed before me,................, a justice of the peace, the....day of ......, 189..

         C—— D——, J. P.

FORM NO. V.

FORM TO BE USED IN THE SETTLEMENT BY THE SHERIFF WITH THE SEVERAL BOARDS OF EDUCATION, ON OR BEFORE THE 30TH DAY OF JUNE IN EACH YEAR.

.........., Sheriff of ....county, in account with the Teachers' Fund of .... district for the year ending June 30, 189..

	DR.	
	$	Cents.
To balance due District on settlement for the year ending June 30, 189		
To amount due from State School Fund for the year ending June 30, 189 ...		
To amount levied on a valuation of $ — for the year ending June 30, 189— at —— cents on each hundred..		
To amount received from other sources for the year ending June 30, 189 .. [Itemize each sum received from "other sources," giving date, amount and from whom received.]		
Total debits....		

	CR.	
	$	Cents.
By balance due sheriff on settlement for the year ending June 30, 189......		
By sundry school orders paid to date.. [The No., date, and name of person to whom each order was drawn, with the actual amount paid thereon by the officer presenting it, should be given in detail.]		
By commission at 5 per cent. on net district levies.........................		
By 2 per cent commission on railroad levy.		
By exonerations—(Name each person exonerated, the name and for what year the exoneration is made)..........		
By delinquent list for the year ending June 30, 189.........................		
Total credits...		
Balance due district (or sheriff, as the case may be)...........		

FORM NO. VI.

CALL FOR SPECIAL MEETING.

OFFICE OF........... ⎫
.... DISTRICT, ⎬
...... COUNTY, W. VA. ⎭
................., 18..

It appearing to .... that a special meeting of the board of education of said district is necessary to transact business relating to .... and other matters, a meeting is hereby called at .... at .... o'clock.... M., ..,...... 189.. You are requested to be present.

....,Secretary.

To ....

FORM NO. VII.

FOR TRANSFER.

.... DISTRICT, ⎫
.... COUNTY, W. VA. ⎬
SUB-DISTRICT, No .... ⎭
...................., 189..

It appearing to the undersigned, trustees of .... sub-district
that ...., children of .... of
...... sub-district are so situated as to be better accommodated in
sub-district no ......, ... district, ... County, W. Va.,
this is to certify that said trustees have this day, as required by
law, transferred them to that district. This transfer is to commence on the .... day of ...., 189.., and continue in
force ...... months.

To the Trustees of Sub- ⎫ .... ⎫
Dist. No.. of.... Dist., ⎬ .... ⎬ *Trustees.*
...... County, W. Va. ⎭ .... ⎭

On the reverse of the transfer (Form VII) the following endorsement may be made:

Transfer of...... scholars from sub-district no...., ...Dis-
trict, ... County, to sub-district no...., ... District, ...
County, W. Va.

We, the trustees of the last named sub-district, this day......
*accept the within transfer in accordance with sec. 12 school law,
.... 189....

.... ⎫
.... ⎬ *Trustees.*
.... ⎭

---

*Or refuse to accept.

NOTE—Trustees accepting transfers from other districts should transmit them to their
board of education, there to be kept on file for the information of the board in making
settlements for the amount due for the transferred pupils
  Trustees making transfers should furnish their board with information of all transfers
made by them, to enable the board to provide for the payment of the pro rata expenses of
the transferred pupils. The following form may be used by the trustees:

To the president of the board of education of........district:

This is to certify that the undersigned, trustees of sub-district
no.., ...District have transferred as required by law ....pupils,
the children of........, from this sub-district to no.., ...Dis-
trict, ...County, to begin on the....day of......, 189 , and
continue ....months.

.... ⎫
.... ⎬ *Trustees.*
.... ⎭

FORM NO. VIII.

FORM OF CONTRACT BETWEEN TRUSTEES AND TEACHER.

This Contract Witnesseth, That,.............,.............., and ·················, trustees of sub-district No. ...... in the district of ...., and county of............, West Virginia, of the first part, having met together as required by section 13 of the School Law, and.............., a teacher holding a No. .... teacher's certificate, and having a certificate of attendance for five days, at a teachers' county institute, held in this State since the first day of June of this year, (or having an excuse for non-attendance at same, properly signed by the Board of examiners), of the second part, have this day agreed that said........ .... shall teach the free school in said sub-district, for the term of........months, commencing on the........day of ...., 189.., for the sum of.........dollars per month, and that for said services, properly rendered, the trustees aforesaid will pay, as prescribed by law, the amount of salary due said ....according to the terms of this contract.

And it is further agreed that if for any legitimate reason the school is not begun on the date mentioned, neither party shall have recourse on the other for damages.

Witness our hands, this .....day of.........., 189..

```
.........................
.........................  } Trustees.
.........................  }
```

.........................Teacher.

FOR NO. IX.

FORM OF COUNTY SUPERINTENDENT'S CERTIFICATE TO THE AUDITOR OF DISTRIBUTION OF STATE FUND FOR HIS COUNTY.

OFFICE COUNTY SUPERINTENDENT FREE SCHOOLS, }
........, ..., COUNTY, W. VA.,........ ...189.. }

To the Auditor of the State of West Virginia.

SIR:—The following shows the apportionment made by me to the several school districts of the county of.............., for the school year commencing July 1st, 189..

Whole amount certified by State Superintendent,.......$........

Amount deducted for salary of County Superintendent, ...

Whole amount distributed to the several school districts, ...

Amount distributed to each school district respectively :

DISTRICTS.	Payment of Sept. 15th.	Payment of Dec. 15th.	Total.
....District, $...........	$.......	$.......	
"	....		
"	....		
"	....		
"	....		
"	....		
"	....		
"	....		
"	....		
"	....		
"	....		
Total, $........			
INDEPENDENT DISTRICTS.			
..............................District, $........	....		
"	....		
"	....		
"	....		
"	....		
"	....		
Total, $.........			

........................, County Superintendent

of....................County.

Section 22 of the School Law requires county superintendents to apportion the State Fund among the several districts of their respective counties and to report the same on this form to the Auditor.

FORM NO. X.

COUNTY SUPERINTENDENT'S CERTIFICATE TO SECRETARIES OF THE AMOUNT OF RAILROAD TAX.

OFFICE COUNTY SUPERINTENDENT FREE SCHOOLS.

To the Sec'y Board of Education of.....................District.
You are hereby notified that the amount due your district for

school purposes and chargeable to the Sheriff on the respective accounts of Teachers' and Building Fund in *proportion to the rate of levy* for each, for the school year ending June 30, 189.., from the................Railroad Company is.............Dollars.
Given under my hand this....day of............., 189....
....
Dated........ ...., 189.. County Sup't.............County.

When the County Superintendent is notified by the Auditor of the amount paid into the treasury by the Railroad Company to the credit of any district for school purposes; or, is notified of the tmount of Railroad tax certified by the Audttor to the Sheriff of ahe County for collection for school purposes, he should, without delay, notify (on this blank,) the Secretaries of the respective Boards of Education of the amount due them from the different Railroad companies that have property in their respective districts. The secretaries of the Boards, when they are notified as above directed, should divide the amounts so reported, between the Teachers' and Building Funds in *proportion to the rate of levy* made for each. The amounts should then be *charged* up to the Sheriff on account of the respective Funds.

FORM NO. XI.

COUNTY SUPERINTENDENT'S CERTIFICATE TO SECRETARIES OF THE AMOUNT OF STATE FUND.

OFFICE OF COUNTY SUPERINTENDENT FREE SCHOOLS.
.............................,189..
To the Secretary of the Board of Education of .... District,
I hereby certify that the amount of State School Fund apportioned to your district for the school year beginning on the 1st day of July, 189.., is ....
.... dollars.
Enumeration for 189.., (corrected)...........................
....
County Superintendent.

This amount will be paid to the sheriff of the county in two equal installments, on September 15th, and on December 15th, next; provided your board levy for a sum, which, together with the balance on hand, funds from other sources, and this State fund, will be sufficient to pay for having the schools of your district taught for at least five months in the year. You will charge the sheriff with the above amount on account of the teachers' fund.
As soon as the county superintendent receives notice from the State Superintendent of the amount apportioned to his county, he should apportion the amount among the respective districts and independent districts, according to the number of youths between 6 and 21 in each, ascertained by the last enumeration, and should

thereupon notify the respective secretaries on this blank (Form 16) without delay.

FORM NO. XII.

Office of Assessor }
OF.......... County. }

To the Secretary of the Board of Education of..........District:

The assessed valuation of the personal property in your district on the first day of January, 189.., aggregates $......

Given under my hand the.... day of ......, 189..

... ., Assessor.

P. O. Address, ...

....

A copy of this notice should be sent to the secretary of each district at the very earliest moment possible, as he must have it on the first Monday in July, at the annual meeting of the board of education.

The assessor of every assessment district shall make out and deliver to the secretary of the board of education of each district and independent school district in his district, on or before the first day of July in each year, a certificate showing the aggregate value of all personal property; and the clerk of the county court shall certify to the said secretary the aggregate value of all real estate in such district or independent school district, which certificates shall serve as a basis for any levy that may be made for school purposes for that year.—(Sec. 43 School Law.)

Any assessor who shall to fail to make out and deliver the certificate mentioned in the forty-third section, and any secretary of a board of education who shall fail to make out and deliver the certificate named in this section, shall be fined twenty dollars, for the benefit of the building fund of the district.—(Part of Sec. 44 School Law.)

FORM NO. XIII.

Office Clerk County Court }
.............County, W. Va. }

To the Secretary Board of Education of.............District.

The assessed valuation of the real estate in your district on the first day of January, 189.., aggregates $............

Given under my hand the........day of..........., 189..

....
Clerk of County Court.

A copy of this notice should be sent to the secretary of each district at the very earliest moment possible, as he must have it at the annual meeting of the board of education on the first Monday in July.

The assessor of every assessment district shall make out and deliver to the secretary of the board of education of each district and independent school district in his district, on or before the first day of July in each year, a certificate showing the aggregate value of all personal property; and the clerk of the county court shall certify to the said secretary the aggregate value of all real estate in such district or independent school district, which certificates shall serve as a basis for any levy that may be made for school purposes for that year. (Section 43 School Law.)

FORM NO. XIV.

COUNTY CLERK'S NOTICE TO SECRETARIES OF DELINQUENT LISTS.

OFFICE CLERK COUNTY COURT }
.... COUNTY. }

To the Secretary Board of Education.................District.

The sheriff of ....county is entitled to credits for the delinquent list (including property erroneously and improperly charged) for the year ending June 30, 189..:

On Real Estate for Teachers' Fund,............. $ ....
On Personal Property for Teachers' Fund,........ $ ....
    Total for Teachers' Fund,................ $ ....

On Real Estate for Building Fund, ... $ ... .
On Personal Property for Building Fund,........ $ ....
    Total for Building Fund,................ $ ... .

You will charge the sheriff with the following amounts, certified by the auditor as paid to the sheriff on account of redemption of delinquent lands paid into the treasury before sale:

For Teachers' Fund,........................... $ ....
For Building Fund,........................ .... $ ....
    Given under my hand the..........day of..........., 189..

....
Clerk of County Court.

The said lists shall be returned to the county court before the first day of July in every year, and the list of real estate shall be examined, corrected and allowed by said court, and a copy thereof certified to the auditor, and another copy to the assessor for future use in making out the next land book. The list of personal property shall also be examined, corrected, and allowed by the court, and the amount thereof so allowed, together with the amount allowed of the list of real estate, shall be certified by the clerk of said court to the secretary of the board of education of the proper district. The original list shall be preserved by the clerk of said court in his office.—*Sec. 48, School Law.*

FORM NO. XV.

SECRETARY'S NOTICE TO COUNTY SUPERINTENDENT, ASSESSOR AND
COUNTY CLERK, OF RATE OF LEVIES.

OFFICE OF SECRETARY BOARD OF EDUCATION.

.........., ..., 189... *To . ... of .... county,
At a meeting of the board of education of .... district
of said county, held on the .... day of ...., 189.., it was
orderded that levies for the support of the free schools of the district for the year beginning the first day of July, 189... be made
for the respective funds at the following rates:

For Teachers' Fund, ... cents on the $100 valuation.
For Building Fund, ... cents on the $100 valuation.

Respectfully,

...................., Secretary.

*Write Assessor, Clerk of Couny Court or County Superintendent as the ca-e may
be. Each must be notified promptly.

SECTION 44 SCHOOL LAW.—Immediately upon the receipt of the
certificate mentioned in the preceding section, and of the notice
from the county superintendent, as hereinafter provided, showing
the amount of the general school fund to which such district, or
independent school district is entitled, it shall be the duty of the
board of education of such district to determine the rate of taxation necessary for the pay of teachers and for the building fund in
their district for the school year and for the payment of any such
existing indebtedness, as aforesaid, and report the same by their
secretary, to the clerk of the county court, to the county superintendent and also to the assessor; and thereupon, it shall be the duty
of the said assessor to extend on his books of assessment for State
and county purposes the amount of taxes levied as aforesaid, in
two separate columns, the one headed "Teachers' Fund," and the
other "Building Fund," from which extension the sheriff shall
proceed to collect the same, and shall account therefor as required
by law. Any assessor who shall fail to make out and deliver the
certificate mentioned in the forty-third section, and any secretary
of a board of education who shall fail to make out and deliver the
certificate named in this section shall be fined twenty dollars, for
the benefit of the Building Fund of the district.

SCHOOL CALENDAR.

JULY.
1. School year begins.
   Member of board takes office.
   (Or before) Assessor certifies value of property.
   (Or before) Sheriff settles with Board of Education.
   (Before 1st day of July) Sheriff reports delinquent property.

1st Monday. Board of Education meets.
   (Or as soon thereafter as practicable) Board of Education lays levies.

1st Wednesday. Presidents meet to appoint examiners.

4. Legal holiday.

3rd Monday. Trustees meet to employ teachers.

20. (Or before) Secretary reports rate of levy.

AUGUST.
1. (Or before) County Superintendent makes report to State Superintendent.

SEPTEMBER.
1. Auditor reports condition of school fund to State Superintendent.

NOVEMBER.
Last Thursday. Thanksgiving Day. Legal holiday.

DECEMBER.
25. Christmas. Legal holiday.

JANUARY.
1. New Year's Day. Legal holiday.
   (Or before) State Superintendent makes report to Governor.

APRIL.
1. (Or before) Teachers make enumeration.

15. (Or before) Secretary transmits copy of enumeration to County Superintendent.

MAY.
1. (Or before) County Superintendent forwards to State Superintendent report of enumeration.

JUNE.
10. (Or before) Auditor notifies State Superintendent of amount of general or distributable school fund.

30. School year ends.

INDEX.